Contributors

Charles S. Benson

Professor of Education. He has also taught at Bowdoin College and Harvard University, and has served as consultant to numerous federal agencies and to state governmental committees in nine states. He has written many books and articles on education and financing matters, and directed the consultant staff that produced the two-volume *Final Report to the Senate Select Committee on School District Finance* (Sacramento, 1972). Professor Benson is presently serving as co-principal investigator, Childhood and Government Project, School of Law.

George F. Break

Professor and Chairman, Department of Economics. He has also taught at Pomona, the University of California, Los Angeles, and Harvard University, and served as consultant to governmental agencies. Professor Break has written widely on fiscal policy at the international, federal, state and local levels, and prepared a staff report for the Advisory Commission on Tax Reform, State of California. The report was published in 1970 by the Institute of Governmental Studies as *Agenda for Local Tax Reform.*

Paul M. Goldfinger

Staff Researcher, Childhood and Government Project, School of Law. He has coauthored research reports for commissions in Maryland and New York, as well as the *Final Report...on School District Finance*, noted above.

E. Gareth Hoachlander

Research Associate, Childhood and Government Project (Finance Division), School of Law. He has also served as a consultant to Princeton University's Outdoor Education Center, and the California Senate Select Committee on School District Finance.

Eugene C. Lee

Director of the Institute of Governmental Studies and Professor of Political Science. He was the first chairman of the Commission on California State Government Organization and Economy, past member of the California Fair Campaign Practices Committee, and formerly Vice President-Executive Assistant of the University of California. He has written books and articles on higher education, state and local government and politics, and local government finance. He is coeditor of *The Challenge of California*, published by Little, Brown and Company in 1970.

Tax and Expenditure Limitation by Constitutional Amendment

FOUR PERSPECTIVES ON THE CALIFORNIA INITIATIVE

Tax and Expenditure Limitation by Constitutional Amendment

FOUR PERSPECTIVES ON THE CALIFORNIA INITIATIVE

Tax and Expenditure Limitation by Constitutional Amendment

FOUR PERSPECTIVES ON THE CALIFORNIA INITIATIVE

by

WILLIAM A. NISKANEN
Graduate School of Public Policy

GEORGE F. BREAK
Department of Economics

CHARLES S. BENSON
School of Education
and
PAUL M. GOLDFINGER
E. GARETH HOACHLANDER
JESSICA S. PERS

ARNOLD J. MELTSNER
Graduate School of Public Policy

with a foreword by
EUGENE C. LEE

1973

INSTITUTE OF GOVERNMENTAL STUDIES | University of California, Berkeley

Library of Congress Cataloging in Publication Data

Tax and expenditure limitation by constitutional amendment: four perspectives on the California initiative, by William A. Niskanen [and others]

1. Finance, Public--California--Law--Addresses, essays, lectures. I. Niskanen, William A., 1933-- II. California. University. Institute of Governmental Studies.
KFC840.A75T38   343'.794'03   73-9974
ISBN 0-87772-170-X

$2.50

Contents

Arnold J. Meltsner

Associate Professor, Graduate School of Public Policy. He has a background in cost analysis, including work with the RAND Corporation, and has written books and articles on city budgeting and school financing reform, including *The Politics of City Revenue*, published in 1971 by the University of California Press.

William A. Niskanen

Professor, Graduate School of Public Policy. He has also taught at the University of Chicago, the University of California, Los Angeles, and the University of Maryland. He has worked for the federal government in the Bureau of Mines, the Treasury Department, the Office of Management and Budget and the Office of the Secretary of Defense, as well as in the Institute for Defense Analysis, and the RAND Corporation. Professor Niskanen has written articles on budgeting, financing and productivity and a book on *Bureaucracy and Representative Government*, published by Aldine in 1971.

Jessica S. Pers

Staff Researcher, Childhood and Government Project, School of Law. She has also worked as research associate and consultant to the New York State Commission on the Quality, Cost and Financing of Elementary and Secondary Education, and as a consultant and editor in the Massachusetts Executive Office of Educational Affairs.

EUGENE C. LEE

Foreword

Sometime during the coming year, Californians will be asked to vote upon a fundamental change in the management of the state's fiscal affairs. Simply put, the change may be posed in the form of two questions:

> Should the authority to determine the level of spending from state tax revenues be transferred from the Governor and the Legislature to the people?
>
> Should the proportion of personal income devoted to state government expenditures (including grants to local government) be reduced?

These are only two of the important issues raised by the Tax and Expenditure Limitations Constitutional Initiative developed by Governor Ronald Reagan and proposed by him in March 1973 for voter approval through the initiative process. The same amendment was also simultaneously introduced into the Legislature as Senate Constitutional Amendment 12, but was defeated in Senate committee on June 13, 1973.

In this symposium, four members of the Berkeley faculty (and in the case of one essay, three research associates in addition) present their views concerning the proposed measure. Following the four essays, William Niskanen (a proponent of the measure) offers a response to the other three authors, whose views turned out to be generally critical. Finally, professors Benson, Break and Meltsner provide brief replies to the Niskanen rebuttal, rounding out the dialogue. The goal of the authors and of the Institute of Governmental Studies in presenting their views is to promote better public understanding of this highly significant proposal.

CONFLICTING VIEWS

To say the least, the initiative is hotly contested. It involves basic questions of political philosophy (the relative role of representative legislative and executive branches vs. the popular institution of the referendum) and economic policy (the appropriate proportions of public vs. private expenditures). In the words of Governor Reagan, the problem is that the people are facing a tax future which will leave them "...defenseless, at the mercy of a vast special-interest oriented government bureaucracy they unwittingly helped to create." The Governor states the proposal will save Californians $118 billion in the next 15 years--money "to keep and spend as they wish...which they otherwise will not have." But in the sharply contrasting opinion of Legislative Analyst A. Alan Post, the initiative will make it almost "inevitable that reductions in state expenditures will be shifted to local governments and cause increases in local property and sales taxes" and that, if fully enacted, California will have to cut the present level of "controllable" state services (i.e., those subject to change in the budget act) by up to 20 percent in less than five years. (Los Angeles *Times*, May 11, 1973).

Both legal language and economic projections are a subject of debate. As reported by Tom Goff of the Los Angeles *Times*, "...to its supporters the plan is 'a perfectly simple and elegant way' to keep government from gobbling up more and more of California paychecks in coming years. To its foes it is ...a 'simplistic scheme' that is 'philosophically, fundamentally and demonstrably wrong.'"

Indeed, the voter has his work cut out for him in deciding where his best long-range interests really lie. But decide he must.

The initiative is extraordinarily important. It involves both short-run and long-range policies and both state and local governments. As such, it will affect every citizen of California. The following paragraphs attempt briefly to summarize the main provisions of the measure, which are subsequently discussed in the four essays. An appendix contains the entire initiative for those wishing to examine the proposal more closely.

A CEILING ON STATE EXPENDITURES

At the heart of the initiative is the proposal that expenditures from state tax revenue (which excludes federal grants and revenue sharing, employment trust funds, user charges, and certain other receipts) shall be limited to their current percentage of State Personal Income, and that this percentage shall decline by one-tenth of one percent (0.1 percent) each year. For example, one estimate is that the ratio for 1973-74 is 8.3 percent. Thus, the limit on state expenditures for 1974-75, the first year of the limitation, would be 8.2 percent. Beginning with 1989-90 or with a year in which the limit is no greater than 7 percent, the Legislature may with a two-thirds vote, eliminate further reductions in the limitation. As a safeguard against an unexpected drop in personal income, a second formula provides that at no time shall the limit be less than the amount of revenue per capita collected in 1973-74, adjusted for inflation.

INCREASES BY STATEWIDE VOTE

The initiative provides that the overall expenditure limitation can be increased or decreased by a majority vote of the people at a statewide election. Such a change can be placed on the ballot by a two-thirds vote of the Legislature or directly by petition of 5 percent of the voters under the initiative process of the State Constitution. Furthermore, the limitation may be increased in order to provide funds for general property tax relief if, at the same time, local government tax rates are decreased commensurately. Other provisions are included to permit specific increases or decreases in the limitation consistent with the general intent of the initiative to maintain an expenditure ceiling.

PERIODIC TAX REFUNDS

While the limitation formally restricts expenditures against state tax revenues, the measure mandates the Legislature to minimize taxes accumulated in excess of the limitation by making periodic tax refunds or reductions from a "tax surplus fund" beyond those funds needed for "emergency situations." The Legislature is required to establish a "special emergency fund" of not more than 0.2 percent of State Personal Income (appropriations to which are also subject to the overall limitation). Upon the declaration by the Governor of an "emergency situation" (i.e., an "extraordinary occurrence requiring unanticipated and immediate expenditures to preserve the health and safety of the people"), the Legislature may appropriate funds to meet the emergency from that fund. If the fund is exhausted, the Legislature may utilize the "tax surplus fund," or may by two-thirds vote authorize a specific tax increase or a new tax to meet the emergency need. However, the special tax may not be continued beyond two years without a majority vote of the electorate.

A TWO-THIRDS MAJORITY FOR LEGISLATIVE CHANGE

A different but exceedingly important thrust of the initiative is the requirement that all new taxes and changes in the rate or base of any existing state tax shall require a two-thirds vote of the Legislature. In contrast, the Legislature may currently adopt tax legislation by a majority vote with the exception of certain taxes on banks, corporations and insurance companies--all of which require a two-thirds vote. In short, the new requirement would make it more difficult to change the existing tax structure than is presently the case. A two-thirds vote of the Legislature would also be required to authorize a local government income tax, while other local government taxes (sales, business license, etc.) are not mentioned and thus remain subject to majority legislative vote requirements.

PROPERTY TAX LIMITS ON LOCAL GOVERNMENTS

At the local government level, the initiative establishes property tax-rate limitations for cities, counties and special districts at the higher of the respective tax rates in effect in 1971-72 or 1972-73. (Statutory law limiting school district tax rates is not affected.) These limitations may be increased or decreased by a vote of the people in the jurisdiction. Local governing boards of these entities may--by four-fifths vote--increase the maximum property tax rate for the purpose of meeting an "emergency situation," but--as with the state--the special tax increase lapses after two years, unless the local electorate votes to continue it. The state (by statute) may also authorize increases in the maximum property tax rates to meet shifts in cost-of-living or population not offset by assessed valuation changes or to allow for "circumstances creating hardship" for local governments.

STATE MUST FUND STATE-MANDATED PROGRAMS

Also affecting local governments, the state is prohibited from mandating to local government a new program or increased level of service under an existing program until an appropriation is made by the state to pay the cost of performing the mandate. There are certain exceptions--for example, workload increases under an existing program or statutes defining a new crime--which are not regarded as "mandated" programs within the meaning of the initiative.

A ONE-TIME TAX REBATE

Finally, the initiative provides for a one-time credit of 20 percent of personal income taxes for 1973 (or 1974 if the initiative becomes effective after December 31, 1973), by use of a substantial portion of the $829 million surplus which is anticipated at the end of the fiscal year 1972-73. On a permanent basis, an across-the-board cut of 7½ percent is established in current income tax liability for 1974 and thereafter. Furthermore, single individuals with adjusted gross incomes of less than $4,000, and married couples and heads of households with adjusted gross incomes of $8,000 or less are exempted from personal income taxation altogether.

CONCLUSION

This, in sum, is the Tax and Expenditure Limitations Initiative upon which the citizen must render a judgment at the ballot box. Should the people, as is argued in the opening essay, restrict their elected officials--legislators and Governor alike--by reserving to themselves the power to fix the overall proportion of their personal income to be used for state expenditures? Or, as is asserted in a markedly different view, is this a shaky solution to an exaggerated problem? In the following pages, we offer facts and opinions on both sides of these questions so that you may come to your own conclusion.

WILLIAM A. NISKANEN

Let the People Decide

Governor Reagan recently proposed an amendment to the Constitution of the State of California that would limit the authority of state officials to determine total state tax revenues. This proposed amendment is the first output of the Governor's "legacy" task forces that are formulating proposals for changes in the structure and processes of government in California. The Governor submitted this proposed amendment for review by the Legislature but, anticipating a negative response, he also initiated a petition campaign to place this proposed amendment on the ballot this fall. This essay summarizes the main provisions of the proposed amendment, the main arguments for the amendment, and some of the issues that have already been raised. As one of the contributors to formulating this proposed amendment, my views should be recognized as those of an informed advocate.

THE PROPOSED AMENDMENT

The central provision of the proposed amendment would establish a limit on total state tax revenues. The primary limit is expressed in terms of a slowly declining percent of total personal income in the state. At the present, total state tax revenues are over 8 percent of total personal income in the state. In each subsequent year, the state tax revenue as a percent of total personal income would decline automatically by 0.1 percent per year until this fraction is reduced to

7 percent or until fiscal 1989-1990, whichever is earlier. By the end of this period, given sustained economic growth, this provision would permit a nearly 200 percent increase in total state revenues and would force a 20 percent reduction in average tax rates. A second limit provision would "recession proof" state tax revenues in the near future; the effective limit, thus, would be the higher of the authorized percent of total personal income or an amount that would maintain real per capita state tax revenues at the fiscal 1974-1975 level.

State revenues subject to the proposed limit include all state taxes and any fees for which the state has a licensing or service monopoly. Major revenue sources exempted from the limit include federal grants, contributions to the employment trust funds, asset sales, and all fees and user charges for services for which the state does not have a monopoly. All revenues from activities of the state university and college systems, for example, are excluded from the limit. One expected effect of the limit provision would be increased reliance on the excluded revenue sources.

The proposed amendment provides two methods for increasing the state tax revenue limit:

1. On declaration of an emergency situation by the Governor, the Legislature may, by a two-thirds vote of both houses, increase state tax rates and/or authorize a new tax that, with other taxes, yields revenues in excess of the limit. Any tax so enacted would remain in effect for at most two years unless its continuation is approved by a majority of the voters in the next general election.

2. At any time, the Legislature may, by a two-thirds vote of both houses, authorize a referendum to increase the state tax revenue limit by a specific dollar amount. Such a change, of course, could also be placed on the ballot as an initiative. Any proposed

increase in the limit, then, must be approved by a majority of the voters at that election.

The primary effect of the tax limit amendment, thus, would be to transfer *one* power from state officials to the voters--the power to determine the maximum state tax revenues. In addition, the proposed amendment increases the legislative vote required on all tax measures from a majority to two-thirds of the members of each house.

The other major provisions of the proposed amendment include one-time tax changes and the major features of SB 90 [Senate Bill No. 90, 1972], the recent school finance-property tax reform legislation. One provision would mandate a credit of 20 percent of 1973 state personal income tax. For 1974 and following, another provision would limit state personal income tax liability to rates no higher than those at present, less a credit of 7½ percent. Both of these provisions would exempt families with annual incomes less than $8,000 from the state personal income tax. Other provisions include limits on local property tax rates, protection of local governments from state mandated costs, and adjustments in the state and local limits for transfer of functions; these provisions have the effect of transforming the major features of SB 90 from a statute to a constitutional amendment.

THE CASE FOR A TAX LIMIT

Over the last two decades, total state revenues in California increased at an annual rate of around 10 percent, while total personal income increased at an annual rate of around 7.5 percent. A continued increase in the state tax share of income cannot long be sustained, recognizing that the total tax revenues in California are now over one-third of state net product.

The primary case for a limitation on total state tax revenues is that each of the groups contributing to decisions on state spending has an incentive to spend more than is valued by the population:

1. The *bureaucracy* has the strongest relative incentive to increase state spending, because this provides for more public jobs, higher salaries, more contract funds, more power and prestige, etc. The power of the state bureaucracy derives from its important role in formulating spending proposals and its monopoly role in supplying state services and information on these services.

2. The *legislature*, as a body, faces most of the political benefits and costs of state spending. Most of the political benefits, however, accrue to the advocates of increased spending, who usually dominate the review committees, and the political costs accrue to all of the legislators. This causes each legislator to advocate spending that specially benefits his constituents and to hope that someone else controls the total level of state spending and taxation. In addition, the processes of vote-trading--the most important advantage of political decision-making by legislatures--inherently leads to overexpansion of state spending.

3. The *governor*, more than any other state official, bears both the political benefits and costs of state spending. Many spending proposals, however, involve costs beyond the Governor's tenure. Any governor, thus, has an incentive to claim the political credit for such spending proposals, the political costs of which accrue partly to his successor.

4. *Private suppliers* of goods and services to the state obviously have a strong incentive to promote state spending, because state spending increases their income more than it does their taxes. The interests of these groups, not surprisingly, are better represented by the Sacramento lobbies than those of consumer and taxpayer groups.

5. *Voters* ultimately receive most of the benefits and bear most of the costs of state spending. There appears, however, to be a differential perception of benefits and costs, primarily because voters do not pay directly some of the major types of state taxes. In addition, some taxes are "exported" to residents and voters of other states. These two effects probably cause voters to approve higher state spending than they would if they recognized and paid directly all state taxes.

None of these conditions, of course, are specific to state government in California. The growing consensus that the federal budget is "out of control" and the current efforts to strengthen the congressional budget process are based on a concern about the same conditions. And the proposed tax limit amendment, by itself, will not change or correct any one of these conditions. *The sole objective of the proposed limit is to constrain the authority of state officials to determine the total state tax revenues.* The proposed tax limit does not eliminate the need to correct these conditions, but it may so constrain state officials that they will address and resolve some of these more fundamental conditions leading to an overexpansion of government spending.

SOME SPECIAL ISSUES

Advocates and critics of the proposed tax limit amendment agree on several points: The proposed tax limit represents a fundamental change in the way we conduct our public business in California, a change that is based on some distrust of the processes of representative government. The main issues, of course, are whether there is reason to be concerned about the processes of representative government, and whether the specific fundamental change represented by the proposed tax limit is desirable. Over the short history of democratic political institutions, proponents of strong government have generally favored representative processes, and proponents of more limited government have generally favored more popular processes. Maybe only historians appreciate the irony that the proponents of limited government and constraints on the representative processes used to be called liberals.

A charge has been made that the ballot is a poor instrument for resolving complex spending and tax issues. I could not agree more. The proposed amendment would transfer only one simple issue from state officials to the voters: "Should the state tax revenue limit be increased by some specific amount?" The Legislature and the Governor maintain the authority to determine the composition of state spending, to set specific tax rates and, of course, to recommend a change in the tax limit for approval by the voters.

Several major areas of disagreement are also obvious: A charge has been made that the advocates of the tax limit presume they know the optimal amount of state revenues. This is incorrect. The proposed tax limit is based on a presumption that the level and the rate of growth of state revenues are too high, but that only the voters have the information and the right to determine the total state tax revenues.

A charge has been made that the proposed two-thirds rule for approving tax legislation, in effect, endorses the present system of taxes. This is incorrect. At present, only the state bank and corporation tax and the insurance tax formally require a two-thirds vote, but most major tax changes have, in fact, been approved by two-thirds or more of the legislators. The proposed two-thirds rule merely assures that all future tax changes are limited to those that reflect broad legislative support.

A charge has been made that the proposed tax limit would increase class conflict in California. This charge must be based on a presumption that the Legislature somehow knows how to ameliorate whatever potential class conflict may exist that would become unnecessarily focused on a ballot measure concerning the tax limit.

In fact, it is far from clear that decisions resulting from the present processes of representative government, on net, reduce potential class conflict. In addition, the proposed amendment--by requiring voter approval of an increase in the state revenue limit--would reduce one major potential source of conflict between the voters and their elected officials. A difference of views on the issue is understandable. The tax limit would contribute toward maintaining voter confidence that the political processes in California serve their general interests.

Advocates of the proposed tax limit may be wrong in believing that the voters in California are dissatisfied with the level and rate of growth of state revenues. The most powerful test of this belief, of course, is whether the voters will approve the proposed amendment. If it is approved, the tax limit amendment would be a reaffirmation of democracy in California and may well provide a model for more direct popular control of government throughout the United States.

A PERSONAL NOTE

The proposed tax limit amendment is the product of a deliberative and consensus-building process involving many people. As such, it is both better and more complex than the submissions by any one individual. It is neither a perfect nor a sufficient instrument to assure responsive government in California. I regret that many legislators rejected the proposed amendment after cursory examination, because a more thorough review may have led to further improvements. Overall, my involvement in formulating this proposed amendment reenforced my belief that complex policy issues are usually best resolved by a deliberative and consensus-building process and that neither politicians nor academicians have any monopoly on wisdom. I urge support of the proposed tax limit amendment on the belief that the voters in California have the information, the intelligence, and the *right* to determine the total state tax revenues.

GEORGE F. BREAK

Economic Aspects: How Real Is the Problem? How Good Is the Solution?

The Governor's "Reasonable Program for Revenue Control and Tax Reduction," (the Blue Book) submitted to the California Legislature on March 12, 1973, is on close inspection less a "reasonable program" than a shaky, pressure-cap solution to a problem whose dimensions have been grossly exaggerated and whose very existence is doubtful. It is no small irony that a Governor who possesses both a line-item veto power and a strong will to use it should feel compelled to call for the mobilization of entirely different kinds of forces in the budget-control battle. Clearly he believes that worries about fiscal matters are widespread and that something rather dramatic ought to be done to allay them. This essay considers first the quantitative importance and basic nature of the problems addressed by the Governor's expenditure-control program, and then turns to the economic effectiveness of the proposed solution.

HOW BIG IS THE PROBLEM?

One of the fundamental arguments put forth by proponents of the Tax and Expenditure Limitations Initiative is summed up in the startling pronouncement that "You pay 44 cents of every dollar in taxes."[1] Close examination, however, shows this 44 percent tax burden ratio to be very insecurely founded. For one thing, the numerator of the ratio (supposedly representing the "tax burden") is padded with items that are neither taxes nor burdens on the payer, such as admission fees to University basketball and football games. For another, the ratio uses a denominator (State Personnel Income) that excludes important items of private taxable income, such as undistributed corporate profits. After making a detailed analysis of the proposition and its many distortions, the Legislative Analyst concluded, "...we find no valid basis for the argument that Californians pay 44 percent of their incomes in federal, state and local taxes.... For the purposes intended it would be far more reasonable to use the 32.6 percent figure of the Tax Foundation."[2] Yet even this latter figure, which applies to the nation as a whole and not to California alone, uses too small a denominator.

What, then, can be said about the taxes Californians really pay in relation to their incomes? Unfortunately for those who like simple explanations, this question has a very complex answer. First and foremost, there is the problem of determining where the burdens of our various taxes ultimately rest. The taxes on corporate profits collected in California, for example, can hardly be said to fall exclusively on Californians, since their burdens undoubtedly extend to many people outside the state who either own shares in the corporations or purchase their products. Conversely, California stockholders and consumers may bear the burdens of corporate profits taxes levied elsewhere.

Similarly, California property tax burdens may be exported to outsiders, and non-California property tax burdens may be imported from other states. Even if economists were in agreement as to the true incidence of all the major taxes, and they are not, it would be a formidable task to make all the allocations required to measure California tax burdens.[3] For the present, then, the best available numerator for the tax burden ratio is the sum of state-local taxes actually collected in California, plus some reasonable allocation of certain federal taxes, such as the corporate profits levy.[4]

The second problem in deriving a realistic tax burden ratio is that of obtaining the correct denominator. Net National Product, the measure used by the Tax Foundation to obtain the 32.6 percent ratio cited above, is clearly better than Personal Income, the measure used to derive the Governor's 44 percent figure. Nevertheless, it still excludes some important kinds of private income that represent just as much ability to pay taxes as any other kind of income. These include government transfer payments to persons, interest paid on government debt, and net capital gains.

In addition, official national income estimates of business depreciation probably exceed true economic depreciation, with the result that Net National Product (NNP) tends to be understated (since income is measured net of depreciation). In the absence of reliable measures of economic depreciation or of net capital gains, we can only adjust NNP partially for its underestimate of total private income. Even this adjustment, however, tends to increase NNP by more than 10 percent. In 1970, for example, when NNP was $890 billion, the addition of government transfers, interest payments and net government subsidies would increase the total income figure to $998 billion. Gross National Product (GNP) in the same year was $976 billion.

These figures, of course, are for the country as a whole. Data for California alone are fortunately available in the form of estimates of Gross State Product (GSP), prepared by the Business Forecasting Project at the University of California, Los Angeles. For the reasons just given, these provide the best choice we have for the denominator of California's tax burden ratio.

When these more accurate figures are used in the calculation of the tax burden ratio for 1969, a far different picture emerges than that presented by the Governor's Task Force. In 1969 GSP was $101.2 billion; for fiscal year 1969-70 total state-local taxes in California were $11.2 billion, split almost equally between the two levels of government; and California's share of 1969 federal taxes, according to the Tax Foundation, was $20.7 billion. The tax-income ratio yielded by these measures is 31.5 percent. Imperfect as this estimate may be, it is far more accurate than the Governor's 44 percent ratio.

An even more startling claim adduced by supporters of the Tax and Expenditure Limitations Initiative is that unless this legislation is enacted, state revenues will increase from $9.8 billion in 1974 to $47.1 billion in 1990, or from 8.75 percent of State Personal Income to 12.3 percent.[5] Enactment of the program, they argue, would limit the increase in state revenues to $27.4 billion and mean a tax saving of nearly $20 billion in 1990.

Such tilting at windmills may have considerable political appeal, but people with a more realistic sense of the probabilities will tend to be less terrified by the fate from which the Governor wishes to save them. One is reminded of the story of the Great Federal Budget Economizer who, exhausted by a long day of saving incalculable amounts of the taxpayers' money, returned home to be greeted by his excited young son. "Daddy, Daddy," said the boy, "I walked all the way home from school and saved the 45-cent bus fare!" Sternly the savings-minded father replied, "Son, such petty economies are wasteful. If you are going to walk all that way, you might at least save a $5 taxi fare."

The Governor's estimates of future revenue are apparently based on a fairly straightforward projection of past trends. They forecast an annual growth rate of 10.3 percent for state taxes during the next 17 years, as compared to an average annual rate of 11.2 percent during the past 13 years.[6] For a number of reasons, however, this seemingly plausible extension of the growth rate is unrealistic and deceptive. Several factors which have contributed significantly to the steep increase in state expenditures during recent years are now abating. Among these are school enrollments (which are declining), attendance at institutions of higher education (now levelling off), and welfare costs (expected to grow at a slower rate and to be increasingly shifted to the federal government). Continued rapid growth in pressure from these sources would indeed, in the words of the Legislative Analyst, require "repeated increases in tax rates,"[7] but realistic projections do not call for such growth. On the contrary, the most reliable and responsible estimates offer a far less gloomy picture of the California taxpayer's future than the one drawn by the Governor.

Of course, it is one thing to argue that California's tax problems have been grossly exaggerated by proponents of the Tax and Expenditure Limitations Initiative, and quite another to conclude that the problems are neither real nor deeply and widely felt. No one could deny the appeal of anticipated tax cuts, but it would be foolish to assume that this tempting objective could be gained without cost. The important question is whether the joys of tax reductions would on balance outweigh the anguish that would result from the inevitable decline of state services.

HOW REAL IS THE PROBLEM?

The basic justification of the Tax and Expenditure Limitations Initiative was succinctly stated by Milton Friedman in response to the question, "Why not reduce government by cutting bad programs?"

> That's a tempting approach. It's one that's been tried over and over again. It never worked, and the reason it has never worked is because, when you take one program by itself, all of the people who have a special interest in that program land in Sacramento like a ton of bricks. It's

> worth their while to spend a great deal of energy on it. On the other hand, the public interest in having that program is diffused. Each one of us saves a few cents, but for the special interests, those cents accumulate into a great many dollars. As a result, whenever you try to take off one special program at a time, the special interests win every time and the general interest is suppressed. The great virtue of this proposal is precisely that it lumps together all of these little programs into one bigger total and, thus, makes it possible for the public interest--that is, your interest and my interest--to be reflected, in the same strength and the same force as the separate special interest.[8]

This is a serious charge against the American political process and should be carefully considered. No one should take lightly the possibility that under the current structure and modus operandi of government the general public interest continually comes out second best in its contest with special interests. On the other hand, no one can prove that this is, or must be, the case. The major alternative possibility is also worth serious consideration.

The other possibility is that the general public interest is indeed well served by existing American governments, but that because of the complex nature of both the public itself and the services provided by government, it is hard to see that this is so. A fundamental feature of public goods, as economists have stressed for some time, is that if their benefits are provided to one person they must be provided simultaneously to all persons. In contrast, the benefits of private goods are confined to the persons purchasing and using them. Recognizing this difference, one can readily see how widespread frustrations over government operations arise. These are the inevitable product of human diversity, and especially the diversity of tastes for public services. No matter what government does, some people will like it, some will be indifferent, and some will be displeased.

Because tastes for public goods are so different, then, each person can have more of the specific benefits that he especially values only by agreeing to allow the government to provide other services which he dislikes but which other individuals value highly. This means that any government program always carries additional costs over and above those of its own operation, for the people who benefit from the one program must pay the price of funding other programs which benefit them little or not at all. In an economic sense, therefore, the public goods market, because of its very nature, must function less efficiently than the private goods market.[9]

Given this reality, it is not implausible to propose the following hypotheses about public attitudes:

1. People will generally regard taxes as being too high. In actuality, however, they are only too high for any individual if they could be reduced mainly, or entirely, at the expense of programs wanted by others, but not by himself. This is clearly impossible.

2. People will generally oppose any comprehensive attempt to reduce government expenditures, at least initially. This is due to the fact that widespread cuts in public services are bound to hurt almost every important group in the community. Therefore people's initial reaction is to attempt the impossible task of sparing their own preferred programs and concentrating the cuts on programs preferred by others. Once the impossibility of achieving this goal is perceived, each group will have the more difficult task of comparing its own public service losses with the tax reductions it could enjoy as a result of the general economy program.

If, under present circumstances, almost every Californian, given the choice, found that he would value the benefits of tax reduction more than the losses in public services, then it would be clear that the problem addressed by the Governor's program has real validity (whether or not his solution to it is the best one available). If, on the other hand, almost every Californian were to miss the lost services more than he enjoyed his additional disposable income, the expenditure limit plan would bring a substantial net loss to the state. In the latter case the Governor's program would be not only unnecessary but positively undesirable. It certainly cannot be proven that this second conclusion is correct, but to say that it is not so bespeaks a remarkable degree of disenchantment with the past effectiveness of the legislative and administrative branches of the state government and with their capacity ever to reflect accurately the general public interest of the people of California.

HOW GOOD IS THE SOLUTION?

While the problem addressed by the Tax and Expenditure Limitations Initiative may seem real enough to many people at this particular time, the solution being proposed needs to be carefully examined. From an economic point of view, two questions especially ought to be asked. Over the long pull, as the economy grows, how effective are the various proposed tax limits likely to be? What structural changes is the program likely to bring about in state-local expenditures and revenues?

Ranked in terms of their potential economic restrictiveness, the three proposed limitations, going from least to most restrictive, are:

1. The State Declining Percentage Expenditure Limitation,

2. Local Entity Maximum Property Tax Rate Limits, and

3. The State Absolute Floor Formula.[10]

This ranking is based on a frequently used standard test for the size of government operations--namely, the extent to which the limits would permit California governments to maintain a constant quality of services in future years. Such maintenance is especially difficult for all government units, because labor productivity tends to rise considerably less rapidly in the public sector than in the private sector. The reason for this is that so many of the most expensive government services are unusually labor-intensive, requiring a high degree of individual attention (e.g., educational, health, and welfare services). Unlike manufacturing industries, for example, the degree to which they can be automated without important sacrifices of quality is relatively limited. The inevitable result of this trend is a steady and continuous rise in the relative price of government services.[11] Translated into terms that every public official will recognize, this means that over time governments have to spend more and more money simply to maintain the same level of output. No doubt some release from this treadmill can be achieved by concerted efforts to improve public sector productivity, but to the extent that quality depends on human services there is no escape from the dilemma. Such services become increasingly expensive as private sector productivity rises. Consequently the public must choose between higher taxes and lower quality government output.

The important question, then, is the extent to which the proposed expenditure limitations will permit such choices to be made by the electorate:

1. Consider first the State Absolute Floor Formula. As its proponents have stated, it is intended to ensure that revenues will always expand to meet the combination of inflation (as measured by the National Consumer Price Index) and population growth.[12] The problem is that these are only two of the three adjustments necessary to permit maintenance of service quality.

The formula completely ignores the productivity adjustment explained above. In other words, even if there were no increases in either consumer prices or population, the costs of a given quality of labor services would rise, in line with increases in private sector labor productivity--at perhaps 3 percent a year. Since labor is an important input in the public sector--57 percent of the cost of state-local output in the U.S. in 1971--government costs would rise accordingly in the absence of offsetting public sector productivity advances. Strict adherence to the State Absolute Floor Formula could therefore be expected to force a continuous reduction in the quality of government services in California.

2. The Local Entity Maximum Property Tax Rate Limits are equally restrictive, and for the same reason, but the proposed legislation would not prevent property tax revenues from rising at a disproportionately rapid rate as long as the growth in assessed valuations outstripped increases in population and in general consumer prices. This would happen only if land and building construction prices rose more rapidly than other prices. As past experience indicates, this is by no means an implausible expection. Furthermore, if state disbursements to local governments were cut back as stringently by the expenditure limit program as they would almost inevitably have to be, considerable pressure would be put on local tax assessors to keep pushing assessments up to the maximum possible levels.

3. Finally, the least restrictive of the three expenditure limitations is the State Declining Percentage Expenditure Limitation. This is less restrictive than the other limitations because it is based on State Personal Income, the growth of which would normally incorporate all three of the forces pushing up the costs of a given quality of government output--i.e., population, price level, and productivity. Nevertheless, it is a *declining* percentage limitation, and while its impact on an average basis might permit modest quality

improvements, it could be much more restrictive for particular programs. The *average* effect would be to force a retardation in the relative growth of state expenditures, and would not at first glance appear overly alarming. If the revenue-income ratio started out at 8.34 percent in 1973-74 and if State Personal Income (SPI) grew at an annual rate of 8 percent, as assumed by the Governor's Task Force, the expenditure limit would grow by 6.7 percent. If, on the other hand, SPI grew at only 7 percent a year, the expenditure limit would increase by 5.7 percent. In either case the permitted growth rate in state expenditures would be 1.3 percentage points below the actual growth rate of SPI.

Determining how this seemingly modest reduction would affect the ability of specific programs to maintain the quality of their services, however, is a complicated matter. If the growth rate of 8 percent in SPI were composed of a 3 percent price increase, a 3 percent productivity increase, and a 2 percent population growth (as the Governor's report projects), the cost of nonlabor services purchased by government would be rising at 3 percent a year, and the cost of labor services at 6 percent. If program workloads rose at the same rate as population, and if program inputs were 60 percent labor and 40 percent nonlabor, constant-quality program costs would be rising at 6.8 percent a year, which is very close to the 6.7 percent increase in the proposed expenditure limit. Too many variables, in other words, are involved in these computations to permit general conclusions to be drawn about the ultimate effects of the limitation even on state-local programs as a whole. The effects on specific programs which the public might be particularly concerned to have maintained at high levels of quality are considerably less predictable.

The final question concerns the probable impact of the Governor's proposal on the structure of state-local expenditures and revenues. Like price and wage controls in the private sector, government expenditure limits are likely to precipitate major changes in the allocation of resources. Some would regard all of these legislated changes as distortions of economic choice. Others (mainly conservatives) would consider only wage and price ceilings as instruments of "distortion." Still others (mainly liberals) would level that charge only at government expenditure limits. Regardless of one's own personal attitudes on this complex question, it is obviously important to know something about the reallocation effects.

The proposed pressure cap is neither tight nor equitable. This is a major conclusion emerging from the Legislative Analyst's examination of the Tax and Expenditure Limitations Initiative. His estimate of $12.32 billion for 1977-78 state expenditures, based on workload projections, suggests at first glance that expenditures would have to be reduced by only 5.5 percent to reach the projected limit for that year of $11.65 billion. In the short run the real crunch, however, would come from the fact that a major portion of total expenditures consists of constitutional and statutory fixed costs. If the required reductions were concentrated on the remaining categories, as is most likely, these "reducible" items would have to be pared by 12.2 percent. Prominent in this sensitive and vulnerable category are expenditures for health, higher education and local schools.[13] Also vulnerable would be local government operations in general, since 68.5 percent of the state budget is made up of local assistance payments.[14] If expenditure reductions in these categories were found to be politically impossible, additional revenues would have to be sought, either outside the limitations imposed by the Governor's program, or in the form of voter-authorized overrides.

Some of the supporters of the "tax reduction" program might be shocked if they were to study the proposed legislation carefully. Like the animals on George Orwell's farm, some of the reductions would be "more equal than others." Some services now financed partially or wholly by tax revenue would undoubtedly be subject to user charges. A prime example would be university tuition. Other budgetary pressures would be met by increases in the relatively few local taxes which could readily be adjusted, such as business license fees. Some of these changes might be much to the liking of many people, but others might cause rather widespread alarm. An ominous note for some, for example, might be struck by one of the primary conclusions of the Legislative Analyst: "Under this initiative it is almost inevitable that reductions in state expenditures will be shifted to local governments and cause increases in local property and sales taxes."[15]

The key to the tax shifts that would probably take place can be found in the varying degrees of stringency attached to the different tax limits in the proposed legislation. Local property tax rates could be increased by a majority vote of the electorate, or for a temporary period in an "emergency" by a four-fifths vote of the local governing body. (This latter provision substantially loosens the tax rate restrictions imposed on local governments by Senate Bill 90, passed in 1972.) The Legislature could by majority vote authorize rate limit overrides for local property taxes, as well as for local sales and other excise taxes. In contrast, local income taxes would become harder than at present to enact, since they could be authorized only by a two-thirds majority of the Legislature. Overrides of all state tax limits would also require a two-thirds vote of the Legislature.

In conclusion, then, it seems clear that the proposed Tax and Expenditure Limitations Initiative is exceedingly complex, and is likely to cause important and highly controversial changes in government operations in this state. Californians for Lower Taxes, unless they pursue that laudable goal with great care and skill, are likely to rediscover an old truth in a new form. Just as there is no free lunch, there is also no cost-free tax reduction program.

NOTES

[1]Political advertisement by Californians for Lower Taxes, San Francisco *Chronicle*, Monday, April 16, 1973, p. 14.

[2]State of California, Legislative Analyst, *An Examination of the Governor's State Expenditure Limitation Program* (Sacramento: April 30, 1973), p. 8.

[3]For an interesting attempt to allocate the burdens of state and local taxes, see Charles E. McLure, Jr., "Tax Exporting in the United States: Estimates for 1962," *National Tax Journal,* 20(1): 49-77 (March 1967).

[4]The Blue Book allocates the corporate profits tax in proportion to California's share of National Personal Income.

[5]Blue Book, p. 39.

[6]Legislative Analyst, note 2 above, p. 13.

[7]Loc. cit.

[8]Blue Book, p. 15.

[9]This is not intended as a full evaluation of the relative merits of private and public markets. Economic efficiency is not the only criterion on which the two should be judged.

[10]The declining percentage limitation is based on State Personal Income (SPI). It requires that estimated revenue be expressed as a percentage of SPI and that this percentage be reduced each year by 0.1 percent. If state revenues in 1973-74, for example, were 8.34 percent of SPI, the limit would be 8.24 percent in 1974-75, 8.14 percent in 1975-76, and so on.

Maximum property tax rate limits are taken over, with some modifications, from Senate Bill 90, which became law in late 1972. They apply to all local government units other than school districts and, in general, allow property tax revenues to increase at least as rapidly as population and prices together.

The State Absolute Floor Formula provides that state per capita expenditure in constant dollar terms must never fall below the actual 1973-74 level.

[11]The classic analysis of this phenomenon is by William J. Baumol, "Macroeconomics of Unbalanced Growth: The Anatomy of Urban Crisis," *American Economic Review*, 57(3): 415-426 (June 1967).

[12]Blue Book, p. 8.

[13]Legislative Analyst, note 2 above, pp. 76-87. The figures cited are based on the assumption that the Governor's proposal for immediate tax relief (SB 238) is not enacted. If it were adopted as proposed, the required reduction in sensitive category expenditures is projected to be 19.9 percent.

[14]Ibid., p. 48.

[15]Ibid., p. i.

CHARLES S. BENSON, PAUL M. GOLDFINGER,
E. GARETH HOACHLANDER, JESSICA S. PERS

Tax Limitation: Is It Worth It?

In a recent Tax Court dispute, a Texan stated that he could not substantiate his income tax deductions because he no longer had his records. Pending a move to a new residence, he had put his records into storage. However, he claimed that because his income tax liability prevented him from paying storage costs, the storage company sold his belongings, including his tax records. The Tax Court considered that a poor excuse. But to a growing number of irate taxpayers, this man's plight is only one example of the tightening squeeze of taxes on personal income.

Certainly public dissatisfaction with government spending is rising. More and more communities refuse to approve increases in local tax rates. One sees recurring newspaper accounts of the elderly pensioner forced to sell his home because he is unable to meet property tax payments. In this connection, California has already moved to protect its senior citizens from burdensome property taxes. Now, Governor Reagan has proposed to protect all taxpayers, by calling for a plan to reduce the percentage of personal income claimed by state and local taxes.

The Governor's proposed Tax and Expenditure Limitations Initiative has at least three points to recommend it. First, in the absence of public approval for an increase in the revenue limit, the program assures taxpayers that they will keep increasingly larger portions of earned income for their personal use than they otherwise would if present government spending trends continued. Placing such a limit on the authority of state officials to determine total state tax revenues may force those officials to examine more closely the claims of special interest groups and agencies that consider self-preservation and expansion more important than effective programs. Another positive effect might be to increase reliance on revenue from those user charges that are not covered by the limitation. Such policies could bring not only existing charges more in line with program costs, but also could provide valuable measures of public demand for state and local services. Finally, the proposed program recognizes ability to pay, at least in a general sense, as one of the most important constraints on taxing policy.

Despite the possible merits of the tax-limit proposal program, there are several potential problems that should be carefully considered before embracing the program as the solution to rising government spending. We will first discuss a number of problems that might arise if the Governor's proposal were adopted. Then, we will look specifically at the proposal's effects on education programs in California. Finally, we will deal with basic notions of the legislative process within a democracy.

PROBLEMS ARISING UNDER THE GOVERNOR'S TAX PROPOSAL

Maintenance of Flow of State Services

Section 12(a) of the initiative proposal is designed to assure that the following statement by Governor Reagan is true: "At no time would state services be allowed to fall below the current level of per capita expenditures, adjusted for inflation and population growth."

The difficulty with the procedure described for determining the State Tax Revenue Limit Population-Inflation Quotient is not hard to find. The measure of price change used, the Consumer Price Index (CPI), is based upon prices of a broad range of goods and services in retail markets. Typically, CPI goes up at a slower rate than do prices of state and local government services. The public sector price index (implicit price deflator for state and local governments) is more influenced by labor costs than is the CPI. Chart I shows the relation clearly.

The difference between the public sector index and the CPI was explained some years ago by William Baumol of Princeton University's economics department. He noted that productivity increases occur unevenly over the components of our economy. They are likely to be low when labor bulks large in the productive process. Conversely, in components of the economy in which physical capital is more important than human capital, technological improvements can increase productivity. State and local government is unusually labor-intensive, even as compared with the federal government, and therefore is largely unaffected by technological advances. Baumol states, "Thus the very progress of the technologically progressive sectors inevitably adds to the costs of the technologically unchanging sectors of the economy, unless somehow the labor markets in these areas can be sealed off and wages held absolutely constant, a most unlikely possibility."[1]

There is a further difficulty with the Governor's "safeguard" intended to maintain the flow of state services. The program stipulates that state services will not be allowed to fall below current expenditures per capita, measured in constant dollars. However, since "current" means 1973-74, it is "current" for only one year. Assuming that there is growth in state revenues and expenditures, what constitutes "current services" in 1985 (measured in constant dollars) could be reduced, though not below the level of 1973-74.

The need for such a reduction in services would come at a time of recession, when income growth falls

CHART I

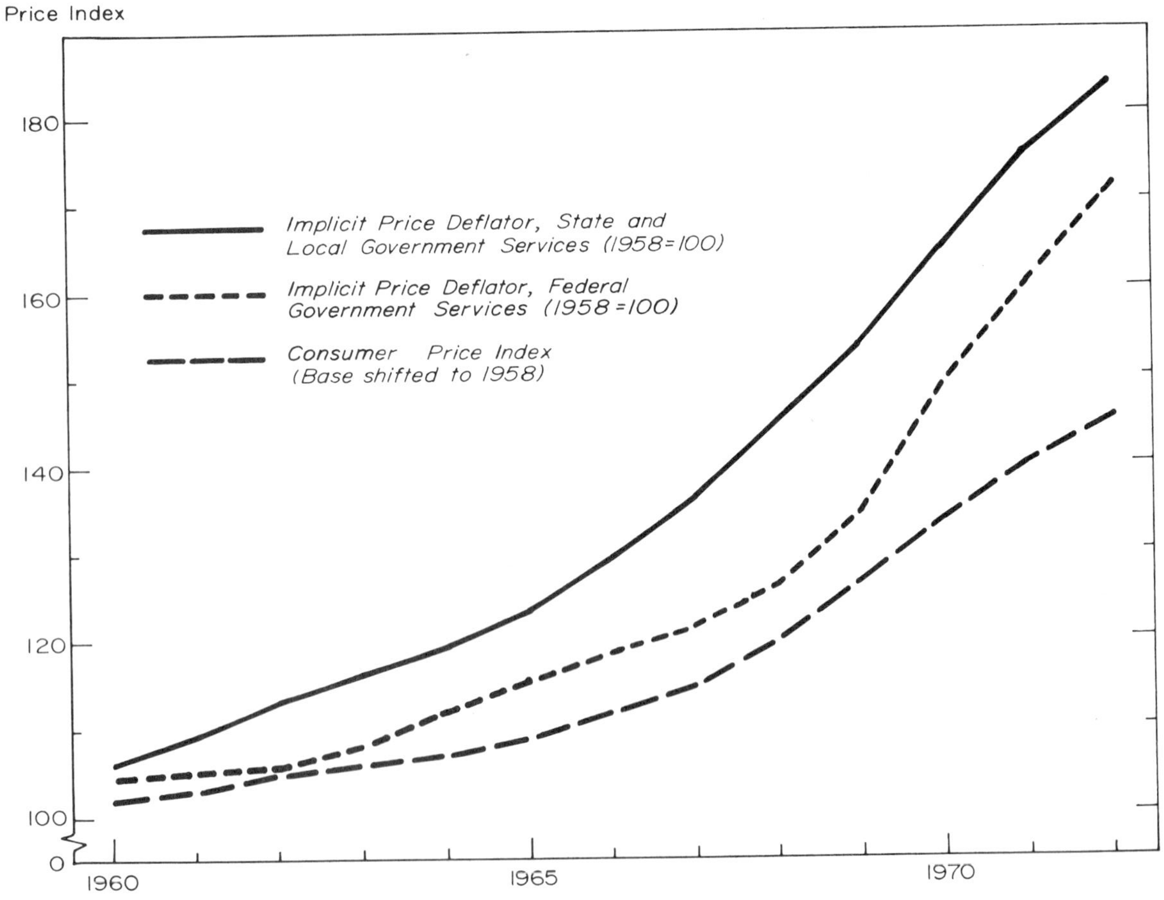

Price Index
180
160
140
120
100
0
1960
1965
1970
Implicit Price Deflator, State and Local Government Services (1958=100)
Implicit Price Deflator, Federal Government Services (1958=100)
Consumer Price Index (Base shifted to 1958)

well below the 8 percent rate assumed in the Tax and Expenditure Limitations Initiative--as it did in 1971, when income growth was only 6 percent. Yet it is in such a recession that increased public services are likely to be required. Therefore, this "safeguard" may provide less and less protection as the base year, 1973-74, recedes into the past.

We conclude: Economic experience indicates that an attempt to safeguard real standards of state service by using the CPI to adjust revenue limits is doomed to failure. The Governor's initiative would establish constitutional mandates that would progressively reduce future real standards of state service.

An Arbitrary Downward Scale

Total annual state revenues now equal about 8.75 percent of Californians' personal income. The proposal would reduce this proportion by 0.1 percent each year until 1990, when the percentage of personal income claimed by state revenues would be rolled back to 7.15 percent. No rationale is offered for choosing either this particular rate of decrease, or the 7.15 percent minimum goal.[2] We are forced to conclude that the choice is arbitrary and bears little or no relationship to projections of public service needs, or to the public's assessment of the value of such services.

The issue in question is not simply what portion of personal income should be devoted to public services. Rather, it is whether the benefits derived from these services are worth what they cost California taxpayers, regardless of whether these costs represent 5 percent, 10 percent, or any other portion of personal income. Arbitrarily setting a revenue limit severs revenue from output considerations.

The plan's proponents claim, however, that the scale is reasonable. They state that, given annual increases of 8 percent in personal income, state government revenues will increase by almost 200 percent in the next 15 years. The actual percentage of revenue increase anticipated is 181 percent. Advocates of the proposal note that revenues would have to increase 118 percent in 15 years to keep even with projected inflation and population growth. The remaining increase (181% - 118% = 63%) will be available for creating new programs and expanding existing ones.

The proponents of the plan imply that this 63 percent revenue "surplus" is a reasonable estimate of the amount required to meet increased demand for public services. It seems overly optimistic, however, to expect that it will be attained under the proposed program. Their estimate assumes the most favorable economic conditions. Consider first their use of the Consumer Price Index as an inflation factor. As was noted above, the public sector price index (for state and local governments) grows faster than the CPI. In fact, since 1958 the public sector price index has grown at an annual rate of 4.4 percent compared with 2.7 percent for the CPI. If the public sector index is used to compute the growth in expenditures necessary to maintain 1973-74 public service levels per capita, expenditures must increase 182 percent by 1990, thus requiring slightly more revenue than that estimated by the plan's proponents.

Furthermore, consider a slightly more unfavorable set of assumptions that might be used to compute the effects of the proposed program. Proponents assume an annual productivity rate of increase of 3 percent. Two factors suggest that this 3 percent figure may be overstated. First, increasing pressures to meet stronger environmental standards may adversely affect productivity. Second, if increasingly larger portions of the labor force move into public employment or the equally labor-intensive private service industries, the result will be an additional downward pressure on overall productivity.

Consequently, if a 2 percent productivity figure is assumed, growth in state revenues would be only 142 percent, or 40 percent short of the amount necessary to maintain the 1973-74 level of per capita public services required, based on computations using the public sector price index. In brief, the proposal is extremely sensitive to changes in public prices and general economic productivity. It would result in a substantial shortage of state funds if economic conditions over the next 15 years are less favorable than those "most favorable" conditions assumed by the plan's proponents.

Twenty Percent Reduction in 1973 State Income Tax

The proposal to use a one-time budget surplus to grant an approximate 20 percent reduction in 1973 state income tax is unconscionable at this time. At the present time, California's income tax burden on middle-income families is low compared to that of other states.[3] But, California will be a high-sales-tax state when the proposed increase in the sales tax rate goes into effect. Traditionally, sales taxes place a heavy burden on middle- and lower-income families. Thus, basic considerations of tax balance and equity argue against the 20 percent income tax reduction. In addition, there are other reasons why we think it is wrong.

1. It is generally agreed that, among major revenue producers, progressive personal income taxes are the most equitable instruments for state governments to use in raising money. In contrast, the state sales tax is not progressive, but at best is a proportional levy. There seems to be an obvious internal contradiction: The tax proposal that purports to be concerned with "ability to pay" actually diminishes use of a progressive personal income tax.

2. One of the intentions of the Nixon administration's federal revenue sharing program is to encourage

the use of state personal income taxes by offering rewards to states moving in that direction. Consequently, the proposed California tax shift could result in a loss of federal funds in this state. At the present time, the magnitude of the loss is too small to be of consequence. However, since the Governor's proposal signals a permanent change in state policy, future increases in federal revenue sharing would be lost to California.

3. Deductions under the federal personal income tax represent the oldest and largest form of federal revenue sharing. Amounts are precisely known; the system works as federal tax law intends. Almost every family knows the amount of state income tax it has paid during the past year. On the contrary, few families know how much they have paid in state sales tax. Thus, state income tax should be stressed above sales tax in order to retain the benefits of federal tax policy for California citizens.

Personal Income as a Measure of State Taxable Capacity

Using personal income to measure state taxable capacity is a bad idea for several reasons:

1. Allocations of wage and salary income of different industries among the states are necessarily only approximate.

2. State personal income estimates do not fully reflect capital gains of California residents.

3. State taxes are levied on economic activity. Personal income, which is essentially an aggregate of household income, is an incomplete measure of a state's economic activity. It would be better to use a measure of Gross State Product.[4]

4. State income is subject to substantial cyclical fluctuations. Since people recognize that government

requires a steady source of income, they are accustomed to seeing their state/local tax burdens rise relative to their incomes in downswings and fall in the ascending part of the business cycle. Such variations argue for using a moving average of estimates of the state's fiscal capacity, rather than relying upon single-year estimates, as the Governor's proposal does.

5. Raising a given amount of state revenue depends upon both tax structure and size of tax base. Using only personal income as a measure of taxable capacity may be misleading, as it ignores the impact and magnitude of total tax burden at various income levels.

Unionism

Organization of public employees is proceeding, spurred by President Nixon's Executive Order 11491, dealing with unionization of federal personnel. A bill is currently before Congress to create a National Public Employees Relations Act, which would extend to non-federal employees collective bargaining rights similar to those held by private sector workers.

The Governor's proposal would force groups of public employees in California to compete for pieces of a pie of fixed size. Therefore, the probable result would be to increase the rapidity with which public workers become organized in this state. In fighting to maintain their shares of the budget, whose total is limited by formula, union leaders would probably feel the need to become increasingly aggressive and to hold desperately onto whatever gains they were able to make. Moreover, because contributions to retirement funds are excluded from state revenue calculations, unions may press for increased retirement benefits and earlier retirement to offset perceived losses in salary increases that are subject to the revenue limitation.

When the Legislature loses the power to set the size of the state's budget, it loses its strength in negotiation. Union leaders may become even less inclined than they now are to exchange workload increases for gains in salaries and fringe benefits. It is entirely conceivable that union pressures will come to dominate the budgetary process. If so, the state will lose the ability and freedom to develop new programs in response to new requirements of the population. This would effectively emasculate the state's highest deliberative body. Recent efforts have been made to raise the capacity of the Legislature to deal effectively with complex and controversial issues. These efforts are beginning to be reflected in legislative performance and correspondingly, in the esteem in which the California body is held across the nation. If union pressures do come to dominate the budgetary process, improvement of the Legislature's deliberative capacity will be of little consequence.

THE TAX LIMITATION PLAN AND PUBLIC EDUCATION

The tax limitation process would probably result in rises in school district property tax rates. Because of the controls placed on the size of the state budget, state grants to school districts could hardly go up at their accustomed rate. Accordingly, the burden of meeting rising school costs would fall on local districts. Authorizing the use of the local income tax by districts, cumbersome as this process would be, would require a 2/3 vote in the Legislature. Increasing local property tax limits requires only a simple majority of the Legislature, and overriding these limits requires only a simple majority of local voters.

Experience with revenue limitation in England has shown that large programs--in terms of expenditures--are especially at risk. Modest adjustments in the budgets of such programs absorb large amounts of funds, ruling out the possibility of increases in many small programs. Therefore, coalitions of interest groups arm themselves to defeat budget increases in large programs and activities. Public education in California, a very large program, is especially vulnerable on this score. It is also locally administered. We conclude that if the iniative proposal is passed the Legislature will be pressed to shift incremental financing of existing public education programs back to the local authorities.

This will result in heavier use of local property taxation, a step backward. Since local school districts are grossly unequal in taxable capacity, the invidious disparities in student support that SB 90 (1972) was intended to correct would quickly reappear.

Poor households in property-poor districts would face unusually onerous burdens for two reasons. First, high local tax rates are needed to raise revenue in poor districts. Second, the deductibility provisions of federal personal income tax laws do not give poor people the same relief that rich people receive.

In higher education, the Governor's proposal can also be expected to produce harmful results. Fees in public institutions are excluded from the limit, and the Legislature would find itself under intolerable pressure to raise fees for tuition and related matters. A major study by Stephen Hoenack contended that rising levels of college fees discourage youth of low-income families not only from attending college but also from completing high school.[5]

In sum, the effects of tax limitation on education appear to run contrary to the goal stated in President Nixon's address to the nation on April 30, 1973: "Equality of opportunity, full opportunity for all Americans."

ASPECTS OF THE LEGISLATIVE PROCESS

One of the basic premises behind the proposed initiative is that government spending cannot be reduced by cutting bad programs. Tax limitation is therefore required.

Public Sector Consumerism

Such an outlook ignores the possibility that "public sector consumer" action could reduce government spending. This kind of consumer action should not be considered farfetched. It is worthwhile to remember that effective private sector consumerism as exemplified by the activity of Ralph Nader and others is a relatively recent phenomenon that seemed impossible a few years ago.

Instead of setting an arbitrary tax limit and forcing competition among the proponents of various governmental programs, we would urge that public-interest accounting groups begin to look carefully at *all* governmental programs and identify policies and practices that are overly costly, duplicative or wasteful. Then, a group of taxpayers (public sector "consumers") could argue for changes in specific programs based on data generated by the accountants. In fact, public sector watchdog activities such as these are getting underway. We believe that this course of action is feasible. Moreover, if pursued vigorously, it could have a powerful and salutory effect on governmental spending and program efficiency.

Legislative Judgment

Supporting public sector consumerism seems to be a more logical use of taxpayer intelligence and initiative than subjecting all tax increases to public referendum. Requiring a referendum before increasing the revenue limit places the average taxpayer in the role of a legislator and forces him to respond to governmental demands without the background knowledge and current information available to legislators.

Legislators are in the unique position of being able to make judgments about diverse and complex program proposals, weighing the potential effects of various schemes and assuring that the needs of all people, including minorities, are protected. Private households, on the other hand, are better equipped to make judgments about whether already functioning programs are working as predicted and providing positive gains. We believe that the Governor's tax proposal mistakenly assumes that private citizens are able to make judgments that are currently and correctly reserved for the Legislature. The role of a responsive and representative legislature is central to our American notion of democracy.

The Use of Referenda

Under the Governor's proposal, California citizens would be allowed to decide on tax rate increases. At first glance, it seems reasonable that citizens should have this kind of control. But on more careful scrutiny, it seems clear that if this initiative is passed many essential programs will not be funded, especially new programs with few committed supporters. If legislators or groups of citizens wish to increase the revenue limit in order to fund additional state programs, they will have to resort to a statewide referendum. Before approving any tax override,voters will probably insist upon knowing precisely how their tax money will be used. Thus, each referendum would have to include a package of programs with corresponding funding levels.

It is unrealistic to expect voters to spend the same amount of time and energy as legislators in understanding the fine details of the various programs in a referendum package. Referenda campaigns will necessarily result in an oversimplification of the issues put before the voters. Under the present system, if legislators approve overly large budgets or costly, ineffective programs, citizens can show their displeasure by voting particular legislators out of office. We believe that this is a more appropriate, useful and desirable check on government expenditures than requiring a statewide referendum on every revenue limit increase.

Protecting Minority Interests

When a package of programs is considered by the Legislature, alternative funding levels are explored; compromises and trade-offs among programs are common. These methods assure passage of many programs that are supported by less-than-the-majority. We fear that such protection of minority interests might disappear if tax increases were subjected to popular vote.

For example, voters currently decide upon expenditure levels in public education. In this area of great local interest and involvement, private citizens can make wise decisions most of the time. However, recent school finance legislation has indicated that the few low-spending, low-taxing districts in California should be spending more on education. Indeed, these districts will be allowed to raise their tax rates so that their expenditures rise to the new foundation levels, without a district-wide popular vote.[6]

Thus, we can see that even on local issues, voters may be overly concerned with taxes, instead of programs. In a statewide referendum we fear that the voter will be more concerned with his individual tax bill than with the interest of *all* the state's citizens. This will be especially true when programs affect only certain localities, ages, or income groups.

Shifting Fiscal Responsibility

Most important, we must recognize that the proposed initiative would control only *state* government revenues, not the total of *state and local* taxes. It cannot guarantee a reduction of the total taxes paid by residents of California. What is almost certain to happen is that the state Legislature will find itself forced to abandon state support of certain existing services, e.g., purchase of school textbooks, in the expectation that local authorities will pick up its bill. As this procedure requires no dollar expenditure by state government, it offers temptations for fiscal irresponsibility. Given the large number of local authorities in existence, most of which cannot well administer any tax except the levy on property, the proposed initiative will have the main effect not of reducing taxes overall, but of shifting the state and local burden to property taxation.

CONCLUSION

The argument presented in this paper proceeded along the following line:

1. Because prices of state and local services will inevitably rise in the coming years, we anticipate that state revenue needs will not be met under the Governor's proposed tax limitation initiative. The section of the initiative that is intended to preserve the real value of services supported by state revenues is unworkable.

2. The consequences of a constitutionally mandated squeeze on state revenues will be unfortunate.

   a. Public employee unions will probably adopt more militant tactics and resist productivity-increasing innovations. This will accentuate the problem of revenue shortage mentioned above. On the other hand, if the revenue limitation is an effective limit on salary benefits, qualified personnel will find the private sector more attractive.

   b. Increased need for revenue to support locally administered services will force local authorities to raise their tax rates. Voting mechanisms imposed in the Governor's proposal make it likely that local property taxation will be inequitable because of the great differences in fiscal capacities of local governments. Under this scheme elementary and secondary education stands especially at risk, because it is locally administered and because it is a very large program.

c. Since user charges are excluded from revenue limitation, the Legislature is likely to demand increased tuition fees in institutions of public higher education in order to raise additional monies.

3. We believe there is a better way to protect ourselves against governmental waste: i.e., consumerism in the public sector. Legislatures are best able to make judgments about the *probable* effectiveness of proposed uses of public money; householders drawn together in politically effective units are best able to judge *actual* program effectiveness. Relying upon the mass of state voters to decide whether various expenditure proposals warrant funding can only produce gross oversimplification of extraordinarily complicated issues and stall the emerging political power of minority members of the population.

NOTES

[1]William J. Baumol, "Macroeconomics of Unbalanced Growth: The Anatomy of Urban Crisis," *American Economic Review*, 57(3): 415-426 (June 1967).

[2]The proposal stipulates that should the tax revenue quotient fall to 7.0 percent prior to 1990, the Legislature may terminate further reductions by two-thirds vote.

[3]Charles S. Benson et al., *Final Report* to the Senate Select Committee on School District Finance, Volume I (California), June 12, 1972.

[4]John W. Kendrick, *Economic Accounts and Their Uses* (New York: McGraw-Hill Book Co., 1972), pp. 200-201.

[5]Stephen A. Hoenack, "Private Demand for Higher Education and the Efficient Allocation of Subsidies to College Students" (unpublished Ph.D. dissertation, Department of Economics, University of California, Berkeley, December 1967).

[6]Both follow-up bills on 1972's SB 90 (Senate Bill No. 90) change the part of §20905g of SB 90 in which low-taxing and low-spending districts were specifically excluded from raising their tax rates without approval of the voters. See 1973 Assembly bills AB 339 (Bagley) and AB 1267 (Gonsalves & Moretti).

ARNOLD J. MELTSNER

The Politics of Tax Limitation

Underlying an apparent technical proposal to control revenue and reduce taxes are strong feelings about the very scope of government itself. The proposal does not define government's scope in terms of specific programs and beneficiaries. Instead it takes an aggregative and distant view, holding that the State of California is now spending about 8 percent of our personal income, whereas about 7 percent would be an appropriate level of spending. Reducing expenditures means that government should do less. Putting aside the proponents' images of an entrenched bureaucracy, special interests, and a vote-trading Legislature, the tax limitation amendment aims at shrinking governmental activity to a lower level than it might otherwise achieve.

Everywhere the proponents look, they see government and its budgets as out of control. In an interview in the April 1973 *California Journal* Governor Reagan expressed this feeling gained from his advisors, "...when this task force on taxes came in with the expert advice that they had from these very noted economists from throughout the country, these men, for the first time in many years, are now of the opinion that government is out of control." The issue of *control* is just another way of putting the question--how much government is enough? No expert can answer that.

While it is dramatic to picture a runaway government, public spending has always been under control. Our budgets are constrained by expectations of the availability of revenue. These expectations come from the willingness of citizens to pay taxes and the political process which anticipates these expectations. Since most of us do not like to pay taxes and politicians worry about what we think, tax increases are constrained.

What the proponents do not like is the political process itself, because it is that process which supposedly increases the budget. By making it difficult for the state Legislature to increase taxes and transferring the site of decision to the electorate, they hope that spending can be held in check. If the voters are contrary and increase taxes, well, that's Democracy for you. Actually, despite the talk about letting the voter decide, voters will not often get into the act after the tax limitation initiative is passed. Most of the time proposed future increases in the limitation will be defeated in one of the houses of the Legislature because of the two-thirds voting requirement to get it on the ballot. A majority voting requirement for the Legislature would have demonstrated the proponents' trust in the public. Nor is it likely that the initiative will be used frequently. The ballot measure confines itself simply to the question of an increase in the limitation. But the motivation for accepting such an increase, that is, what it might buy, will be buried in the confusion of the campaign. Hence, few will pay for the expense of getting a tax increase on the ballot.

Like other governments, our state government is inefficient and imperfect. Since government is a reflection of ourselves, who would expect otherwise? As citizens we expect the government to emphasize distribution of services. We want the major highway built to our city, or we want the lake stocked with fish. Seldom do we worry about how to pay for the various services we all want. Tax decisions, for most of us, are separated from spending decisions. If the two decisions were tightly connected, then no one would be worrying about a runaway budget. Some of us would be getting services which others of us paid for, but we would all know about it. Instead, for both citizen and official, there is little connection between taxes and expenditures.

The tax limitation proposal "corrects" this situation by making it worse. Its proponents, advocates of the private sector and enlightened choice, do not suggest such illumination for the public sector. Rather than creating a nexus between taxes and expenditures, the proposal attenuates what little connection there is now. It does not tell us what service we will give up in the future--that is the Legislature's worry. Avoiding programmatic considerations makes it easier to cut taxes. The proposal makes it appear that we can pay less and get more.

But some of us will get less. It is not easy to pinpoint exactly which citizens will gain and which will lose. One thing is clear: New programs to serve new constituencies will have a hard time. The designers of the tax limitation proposal feel that by setting a ceiling, public officials will have an incentive to reallocate their resources. No doubt small reallocations will take place and small efficiencies may be achieved. Large reallocations are not possible because the proposal does nothing to alter the political forces that created the structure of expenditures we now have. The Legislature, which has been criticized for supinely responding to "special interests," has not been given the political support by the amendment's proponents to disengage from old demands. Instead the Legislature and the executive will have an excuse for displacing new demands on other units of government.

For the most part, officials will be reluctant to open up old controversies, so past decisions will keep most present allocations intact. There are a few interesting exceptions. Consider the exclusion of some fees and user charges from the revenue limitation. To free money for other purposes, the Legislature and Governor will have an incentive to encourage agencies to live on their fees. Rather than setting fees to regulate and encourage use, fees will have to be set to recover costs. Users of the state parks may find it cheaper to go to Disneyland. The revenue of the state university and college system is also excluded, which means that higher tuition charges are likely. Now, personally, I favor the use of tuitions but only if coupled with some program of loans and scholarships that provide a measure of equal opportunity. But where will the money for scholarships come from? Living under the limitation, the state will not cough up extra funds nor can we expect students to pay for each other by their tuitions. Under such conditions, we will have a public higher education system which is not accessible to the public.

Policies, when first conceived, are sure to be imperfectly designed. And the limitation proposal is no exception. To have a limit on spending or a control is not such a bad idea. After all, planning and annual budgeting activities could benefit from having a target figure. Having the control with its supporting language, however, locked into the state Constitution is another matter. The detailed language of policy has a way of backfiring. In one section (4b), for example, the proposal exempts some lower income citizens from having to pay state income tax: a worthy objective indeed, but unfortunately by using the words "adjusted gross income" it will allow a number of wealthy citizens to also escape paying any state income tax.

Then there are the sections (9a, 10a) which deal with adjustments to the limitation due to changes in property tax relief. The general idea behind these provisions is to encourage property tax relief, but the language could actually discourage property tax relief for some of us. As the Legislative Analyst pointed out in his report, adjustments to the limitation are for payments to local governments and not to individuals.[1]

One supposes that only in desperation would the Legislature take back existing relief to individuals, such as senior citizens and renters. But certainly the Legislature would not increase its direct property tax relief to senior citizens because such relief does not qualify for a corresponding increase in the limitation on expenditures. The proposal makes it difficult to target property tax relief where it may be most needed, whether to senior citizens or businessmen.

All of the above imperfections could have been remedied if the proponents had allowed the usual governmental, executive and legislative processes to operate. By making the amendment a constitutional issue, by resorting to an initiative, and by distrusting the very process of which they are a part, the proponents lost the corrective action of the policy process. The voters will be asked to choose, but they will not be able to respond with the required corrections, only an unqualified yes or no.

What's the political feasibility of the proposal? In its current form the Legislature is not likely to put it on the ballot, but once in the hands of the voters, it might pass. For one thing the proposal has been packaged with some skill. Tying the limitations to the refund is a shrewd tactic. Moreover, the timing of the proponents is excellent. With the "failure" of many federal social programs and a growing skepticism about our political institutions, liberals may feel it appropriate to limit the scope of government. Take a number of these disgruntled liberals, add the taxpayers who want to get part of their money back, throw in a dash of conservative voters, and one has a recipe for success. Once passed, Californians will be living with the limitation's debilitating consequences for a long time. At least, this is obviously what the proponents hope.

NOTE

[1]State of California, Legislative Analyst, *An Examination of the Governor's State Expenditure Limitation Program* (Sacramento: April 30, 1973), pp. 41-44.

WILLIAM A. NISKANEN

A Response to the Critics

THE ADVERTISED CLAIMS

A major part of the essay by George Break, interestingly, bears on the promotional claims for the tax limit amendment, and not on the substantive proposal:

1. A newspaper advertisement endorsing the tax limit claimed that "You pay 44 cents of every dollar in taxes." This estimate was based on the broadest available measures of government revenue and income specific to California. Break contends that this claim overstates the relative tax burden in California, although there are no state-specific data on which to base a more accurate estimate. I agree. Total government revenues in the United States are now 35 percent of Net National Product. Some small part of government revenues are from nontax sources, but California tax rates are higher than average, so the total taxes paid by California residents are probably around 35 percent of Net State Product. The primary issue, however, is not whether 44 percent or some other number is the most accurate estimate of the relative tax burden but whether the actual tax burden is too high. Advocates of the tax limit amendment believe the tax burden is too high, and have proposed a procedure to permit California voters to express directly their views on this matter.

2. The tax limit "Blue Book" claimed that a continuation of the rate of increase of state revenues in California would yield total revenues of $47 billion in

1990, $20 billion more than would be permitted by the tax limit. Break contends that this estimate overstates the probable growth of state revenues and, thus, the "savings" due to the tax limit, because of expected reductions in the rate of increase of state spending for schools, higher education, and welfare.

Break may be right, but I think he underestimates the ability of public officials to discover new "unmet needs." In any case, he can't have it both ways. If state revenues would not otherwise increase as fast in the future because of a lower rate of increase of "workloads" demands, the tax limit amendment would "save" less but would also provide ample funds for new programs. A recent projection of aggregate state and local finances in the nation, based on the historical rate of increase of tax revenues and of spending per unit of workload, indicates an aggregate annual surplus of around $26 billion by 1980.[1] The tax limit amendment would assure that most of the California part of this projected surplus is translated into tax reductions rather than new programs, unless the voters in this state decide otherwise.

One does not expect a distinguished scholar to endorse a proposed policy on the basis of its advertised claims. I am a bit surprised that Break seems to reject the tax limit amendment because the advertised claims of this recognizably complex issue are dramatically simplified.

THE CRITICS' CLAIMS

For symmetry at least, two of the critics' simplified claims about the effects of the tax limit amendment should not go unchallenged:

1. The essays by both Break and by Benson et al. claim that the tax limit amendment would cause an "inevitable decline in state services" except under "the most favorable economic conditions." Break's estimate

that "constant-quality program costs would be rising at 6.8 percent a year," very close to the revenue increase permitted by the tax limit, assumes that (1) workload demands will increase at a rate equal to the rate of population growth and (2) a *zero* rate of increase of productivity of state employees. Break's own discussion challenges the first assumption, based on an expectation of conditions that will reduce the rate of increase of school enrollment and the welfare population. The second assumption, distressingly, is more consistent with the evidence, but is in no sense inevitable.

Benson et al. estimate that dollar spending for present programs would have to increase by 182 percent by 1990, essentially the same as provided by the tax limit, if there is a sustained increase in the productivity of the private sector. Their estimate assumes that (1) workload demands will increase at a rate equal to the rate of population growth and (2) the state and local price index will continue to increase relative to consumer prices at the proportionate rate experienced since 1958. The rapid recent increase in the relative price of state and local services, however, occurred during a period of rapid increases in state and local employment. A reduction in the rate of increase in workload demands, however, should reduce the rate of increase of state and local employment, and the relative price of state and local services should therefore not continue to increase at the recent ratio.

Benson et al. also claim that a reduction in the rate of increase of productivity would cause a severe revenue crunch, without pointing out that this reduction would probably cause a lower rate of state and local wage increases. One interesting condition neglected in both essays: The cost of those state and local services that are strictly "public goods" should be unaffected by the projected increase in the state's population.

2. Benson et al. claim that the tax limit amendment would reduce the bargaining power of the state relative to its employees. Any theory and evidence about

bargaining with which I am familiar suggest just the contrary: The bargaining power of a group is *strengthened* by limiting the amount of their possible concessions. Indeed, one of the primary effects of the tax limit amendment may be to prevent most of the increase in state revenues from being absorbed in wage increases.

All in all, it appears that some of the critics' claims may also be dramatically simplified.

THE ALTERNATIVES

Several alternatives to increase the responsiveness and efficiency of state government are suggested by critics of the tax limit amendment and deserve comment:

1. Benson et al. suggest that "'public sector consumer' action could reduce government spending." This suggestion seems analogous to an exhortation for people to be saints, relying, as it does, on the potential for private provision of a public good. A population of Kantian saints, of course, would have no need for government at all. This suggestion overlooks the point made forcefully by Mancur Olson that, given the organizational costs of voluntary collective activity, people have a much greater incentive to organize to further their special interests as producers and governmental beneficiaries than to further their general interests as consumers and taxpayers.

2. Benson et al. also suggest that "voting particular legislators out of office...is a more appropriate, useful, and desirable check on government expenditures than requiring a statewide referendum on every revenue limit increase." If this traditional process were sufficient, there would be no basis for any current concern about government spending. Any voter, however, has an opportunity to vote for or against only those legislators from districts of which the voter is a resident. How can a voter vote against a legislator from another district who has increased state spending for his

constituency? Why should a voter vote against a legislator from his own district who has increased state spending for his constituency? Most of the Legislature, of course, consists of just such men. This suggestion overlooks the condition that, within the legislatures, spending control is a "public good" and, in the absence of some collective action such as the tax limit amendment, will be undersupplied.

3. Meltsner suggests that "a limit on spending or a control is not such a bad idea," but he prefers one selected by public officials to one "locked into the state Constitution." I would be more enthusiastic about this suggestion if (1) there was any evidence of the efficacy of such legislatively imposed controls, and (2) there was a broader recognition among California legislators of the desirability of such controls. The record of federal outlay and debt limits, however, suggests that such limits are either not constraining or are vulnerable to the pressures that make the controls desirable. The strong adverse reaction to the tax limit amendment by leading California legislators, without proposing any alternative, suggests that there is not yet a sufficient recognition of the desirability of some control mechanism to establish and enforce a legislatively imposed spending or revenue control.

A constitutional limit on state revenues is recognizably a new idea, without any history on which to base an estimate of its effectiveness. I suggest that it deserves a trial.

NOTE

[1] American Enterprise Institute, Long-Range Budget Project.

GEORGE F. BREAK, CHARLES S. BENSON et al.,
ARNOLD J. MELTSNER

The Critics Reply

Response by George F. Break

It is interesting and even amusing to compare Professor Niskanen's rebuttal of my analysis with his own original paper. The rebuttal dismisses my appraisal of the economic basis and implications of the proposal as dealing with "promotional claims." He even agrees with me that the 44 percent figure "overstates the relative tax burden" and implies that such details are unimportant. Yet Niskanen's own paper introduces his "Case for a Tax Limit" with a description of this self-same, horrendous tax burden. In his original draft (later changed) he used the slightly slimmed-down figure of 42 percent to describe that burden. The edited draft reduced it to more general terms, and in his rebuttal the burden has assumed the relatively svelte size of 35 percent and is pushed aside as unimportant.

Unfortunately for any economist attempting to analyze the Governor's proposal, all the supposed statistical evidence provided to sustain it disappears into the slippery ooze which underlies the whole scheme. Niskanen's rebuttal again illustrates this phenomenon when he brushes aside my analysis of the original "Blue Book" claim that this limitation would save the state almost $20 billion by 1990. If this, too, is merely a "promotional claim," then what in the world is this proposal all about? If the tax burden is really not so very great after all, and if the estimates of future massive increases are really just advertisers' claims, then why must the basic structure of California government be changed to remove so much discretionary power in budgetary matters from the state's elected representatives?

The fact is that the only thing the proponents of this essentially dangerous and undemocratic program have to go on is a general philosophical conviction that the democratic process is too expensive. Friedman has spelled this out in the statement which I quoted in my paper. Niskanen himself deals, both in his paper and in his rebuttal, not with defensible economic evidence but almost entirely with ideological generalizations. It is always fascinating to find extreme conservatives joining the radical left in their desire to save American government from elected representatives and return the power to the people. Whereas this means for the left substituting a kind of mobocracy for representative government, it means for the right rigidly restricting government's power to redistribute resources.

Advocates of this proposal, including Niskanen, place much emphasis on the sanctity of "popular" democracy, in contradistinction to the suspect representative kind. Evidently in this case "popular" democracy consists of selling this limitation scheme to a confused public by the use of egregiously and admittedly false "advertisers' claims." A majority vote, so gained, could tie up the state tax system in such a way that a two-thirds vote of the Legislature would be required to increase the rate of any state tax (and not just the bank and corporation tax, as at present); furthermore, even a unanimous Legislature could not, without the Governor's approval, exceed an arbitrary expenditure limit, no matter what the needs of the state. (Ironically, conservatives might discover this "maximum" becoming a de facto "minimum" as time and custom hardened the lines.) This marvelous act of "popular" democracy would turn over sole discretion to one person, the Governor, in deciding whether an "emergency" situation existed and the limits might temporarily be eased. It would remove the onus of decision from local representatives who relatively easily can be seen, written to, reelected, or removed from office. The tools of democracy would be safely placed on a high shelf, out of the reach of the little folk who might be injured by playing with them.

Plebiscite democracy--"Do you want limits on state expenditures--yes or no?"--always appeals to those who fear that the electoral process cannot be trusted. Paradoxically they always defend their case with strong protestations of love for the "people."

Governor Reagan calls this initiative "A once-in-a-lifetime opportunity." If it is voted in, the opportunity to achieve fiscal flexibility at the state level will not soon arise again.

Response by Charles S. Benson, Paul M. Goldfinger, E. Gareth Hoachlander and Jessica S. Pers

Professor Niskanen questions our use of a state and local price index and our assumption of a decrease in economic productivity. The public price index is affected by private sector productivity, public sector productivity, and changes in consumer prices. Economic theory suggests that a decrease in private sector productivity would narrow the gap between the public sector price index and the Consumer Price Index, provided there were no corresponding decrease in public sector productivity. Unfortunately, there has been little empirical investigation to determine the exact nature of the relationship between these variables. Consequently, we cannot predict precisely the effect of a decrease in private sector productivity on the public price index.

We can, however, examine the tax limit proposal's sensitivity to changes in these variables. In making their computations, the initiative's proponents use the historical trend in private sector productivity, but choose to neglect the historical trend in state and local prices. The result is a 63 percent surplus available for new programs. But if the historical trend in both variables is used, the surplus disappears completely.

Finally, if the proponent's assumptions are reversed, and the historical trend in public prices is used, but the trend in productivity is changed, calculations produce a revenue shortage of 40 percent. No one, of course, can say with certainty what the future pattern will be. However, since the proposal is very sensitive to changes in productivity and the state and local price index, we believe that it is unwise to adopt permanently a plan that reduces the state's ability to cope with unknown future changes in these economic variables.

Response by Arnold J. Meltsner

As any good conservative knows, workable political institutions develop slowly. They adapt to social change with caution. What we have now, while imperfect, may be better than what we might have. If legislators are not in favor of a control on expenditures, as Niskanen suggests, it is probably because they perceive the Governor's proposal as being too drastic and damaging a change in existing political arrangements. Discussion about the efficacy of controls, in general, will take place among our public officials when the climate of distrust of our political institutions has dissipated. Unfortunately, the issue of controls was articulated in such a hostile, antigovernment manner that, for the present, fruitful discussion is not possible.

APPENDIX

Text of the Initiative: Tax and Expenditure Limitations

INITIATIVE MEASURE TO BE SUBMITTED DIRECTLY TO THE ELECTORS

The Attorney General has prepared a title and summary of the chief purposes and points of the proposed measure, as follows:

TAX AND EXPENDITURE LIMITATIONS. Initiative Constitutional Amendment. Limits State expenditures; restricts use of defined surplus revenue to tax reductions, refunds, or emergencies. Eliminates personal income tax for lower income persons; reduces others' 1973 or 1974 tax up to 20%, from surplus, and subsequent year rates 7½%. Requires two-thirds legislative vote for new or changed State taxes. Limits local property tax rates except school districts'. Requires State funding of new programs mandated to local governments. Provides for tax and expenditure limit adjustments when functions transferred. Contains special indebtedness obligation provisions. Allows local tax rate and expenditure limit increases upon voter approval. If the proposed initiative is adopted undefined additional financing from State sources in the approximate amount of Five Hundred Sixty Eight Thousand dollars ($568,000) on a one-time basis and Two Hundred Thirty Six Thousand dollars ($236,000) annually thereafter will be required for State administrative costs.

To Honorable Secretary of State of California:

The undersigned hereby proposes that the Constitution of the State of California be amended by adding Article XXIX and petitions the Secretary of State to submit this proposal to the electors of California for adoption. The text of the proposed measure is as follows:

"The People of the State of California do enact as follows:

"The Constitution of the State of California is amended by adding Article XXIX, to read:

ARTICLE XXIX
REVENUE CONTROL AND TAX REDUCTION

SECTION 1. Declaration of Purpose.

The people of the State of California declare it is in the best interests of the State to effect an orderly reduction of their tax burden, without shifting costs to local government, by enacting this Constitutional provision to:

(a) Limit and reduce State taxes,

(b) Provide for refunds to the taxpayers of surplus State revenues,

(c) Limit Local Entity property tax rates,

(d) Establish funding procedures for Emergency Situations, and

(e) Require voter approval of taxes which exceed the limits set forth in this Article.

SECTION 2. State Tax Revenue Limit; Tax Surplus Fund; 20% Tax Refund.

(a) There is a State Tax Revenue Limit determined as provided in this Article.

(1) If State Tax Revenues for any fiscal year exceed the State Tax Revenue Limit for that fiscal year, the excess shall be transferred to the Tax Surplus Fund, which is hereby established.

(2) The Tax Surplus Fund shall be used only for one or more of the following purposes:

(i) For tax refunds or reductions;

(ii) For approved Emergency Situation appropriations under Section 6 of this Article.

(3) The Legislature shall minimize accumulations within the Tax Surplus Fund by making periodic tax refunds or reductions as permitted by this Article.

(b) On the effective date of this Article, the Controller shall determine the amount of surplus in the General Fund as of the end of fiscal year 1972-73 and shall designate such portion of the surplus as is necessary and available to effect the refund of subdivision (b) (1) hereof.

(1) The surplus so designated shall be utilized for a refund by means of a credit of 20% of personal income taxes for the calendar year 1973, excluding taxes on capital gains on assets held for more than one year, items of tax preference, estates and trusts, or in such lesser percentage as the Director of the Department of Finance shall certify is available for such refund. Single individuals whose adjusted gross income is less than $4,000.00 and married couples and heads of households whose adjusted gross income is less than $8,000.00 shall bear no personal income tax. If this Article is effective on or before December 31, 1973, then this paragraph shall apply to the 1973 taxable year. If this Article becomes effective after December 31, 1973, then this Section shall apply to the 1974 taxable year.

(2) If, prior to the effective date of this Article, a statute is enacted providing the refund as set forth in subdivision (b) (1) of this Section, such statute shall be deemed compliance with the requirements of this subdivision (b) to the extent such refund is provided.

(3) The Legislature shall, by statute, implement the tax refund required by subdivision (b) (1)as to application to non-resident and fiscal year taxpayers and as to credits in computing liability.

(4) State Tax Revenue for purposes of computing the State Tax Revenue Limit as here defined shall not be reduced by refunds made pursuant to this subdivision (b).

SECTION 3. Appropriation Limit.

No appropriation shall cause an expenditure during any fiscal year of State Tax Revenues for that fiscal year in excess of the State Tax Revenue Limit for that fiscal year, other than for tax refunds or, pursuant to Section 6 of this Article, for Emergency Situations. Subject only to such exceptions, any such expenditure in excess of the State Tax Revenue Limit is prohibited. The Legislature shall, prior to any other appropriation, first make provision for the payment of the principal and interest on the indebtedness of the State.

SECTION 4. State Tax Adjustments; Personal Income Tax Reduction.

(a) The imposition of any new tax or the change in the rate or base of any tax by the Legislature shall be by statute passed by roll-call vote entered in the journal, two-thirds of the membership of each house concurring, except for tax refunds or reductions by appropriations specifically declared to be out of the Tax Surplus Fund which shall be by statute passed by a vote of the majority of the membership of each house.

(b) For 1974 and thereafter, the State personal income tax liability of taxpayers shall be determined at rates no higher than those in effect on January 1, 1973, less a credit of 7½%. Single individuals whose adjusted gross income is less than $4,000.00 and married couples and heads of households whose adjusted gross income is less than $8,000.00 shall bear no State personal income tax. The Legislature shall, by statute, implement the tax reduction required by this Section as to application to non-resident and fiscal year taxpayers and as to credits in computing liability. The provisions of this subdivision (b) may be modified by statute passed by roll-call vote entered in the journal, two-thirds of the membership of each house concurring. If this Article becomes effective after December 31, 1973, then this subdivision shall apply to 1975 and thereafter instead of 1974 and thereafter.

SECTION 5. State Tax Revenue Limit Adjustment by Election.

The State Tax Revenue Limit may be increased or decreased by a designated dollar amount by a majority vote of the people at a Statewide election approving a measure placed on the ballot by the Legislature by a roll-call vote entered into the journal, two-thirds of the membership of each house concurring, or placed on the ballot as an initiative statute pursuant to Article IV of this Constitution. A measure so approved shall take effect the day after the election, unless the measure provides otherwise.

SECTION 6. Emergency Fund and Emergency Appropriations.

(a) A Special Emergency Fund of not more than 0.2% of the State Personal Income shall be established and maintained by the Legislature. Money appropriated to the Special Emergency Fund shall be from State Tax Revenues and shall be subject to the State Tax Revenue Limit.

(b) Upon the Governor's declaration of an Emergency Situation and the exhaustion of such emergency funds as may be available from the Federal Government, the Legislature may make appropriations to meet the Emergency Situation from the Special Emergency Fund or, if that fund is exhausted, either from the Tax Surplus Fund or from State Tax Revenues derived from a specific tax increase or a specific new tax designated for the Emergency Situation and enacted in accordance with Section 4 of this Article. Any tax so enacted shall remain in effect no longer than two years, unless its continuation is approved by a majority of the votes cast for and against its continuance at a Statewide election.

SECTION 7. Local Taxes.

(a) The Maximum Property Tax Rates of each Local Entity are set at the rates levied for the fiscal year 1971-72 or for the fiscal year 1972-73, whichever is the higher. The Maximum Property Tax Rates for a Local Entity created after the effective date of this Article shall be established by the electorate of the Local Entity at the time of its creation.

(b) To permit adjustment of the Maximum Property Tax Rates set in subdivision (a) of this Section, the Legislature shall enact statutes, within the general intent of this Article, to permit:

(1) Maximum Property Tax Rates to be increased or decreased to reflect cost variations due to cost-of-living or population changes not offset by assessed valuation changes or to allow for other special circumstances creating hardship for individual Local Entities.

(2) Maximum Property Tax Rates to be increased or decreased when authorized by the electorate of the Local Entity, or if there is no electorate, then as provided by the Legislature.

(3) Maximum Property Tax Rates to be increased by a four-fifths vote of the governing board of a Local Entity, to secure revenue to defray the costs of an Emergency Situation affecting the Local Entity, but any such increase shall remain in effect no longer than two years, unless its continuation is approved by the Local Entity's electorate.

(c) All property taxable by Local Entities and School Districts, except personal property specially classified for the purpose of assessment and taxation pursuant to the provisions of Section 14 of Article XIII of this Constitution, shall be assessed at a uniform percentage of full value established by the Legislature. If that percentage is any figure other than twenty-five, the maximum rates prescribed in subdivisions (a) and (b) of this Section shall be converted into new maximums by multiplying them by twenty-five and dividing them by the new assessment percentage. Full value, as used herein, means fair market value or such other standard of value as is required or authorized under this Constitution.

(d) No Local Entity or School District shall impose, levy or collect any tax upon or measured by income, or any part thereof, except as authorized by the Legislature by a statute passed by a roll-call vote entered in the journal, two-thirds of the membership of each house concurring. This subdivision (d) shall not be construed to prohibit the imposition, levy or collection of any otherwise authorized license tax upon a business measured by or according to gross receipts.

SECTION 8. Protection of Local Entities and School Districts from State-Imposed Costs.

(a) After the effective date of this Article, no new program, or increase in level of service under an existing program, shall be mandated to Local Entities or School Districts by the State until an appropriation has been made to pay to the Local Entities or School Districts the costs of the mandated program or service, but no appropriation for payments to Local Entities or School Districts shall be required if such program or increase in level of service under a program is determined by the Legislature to be applicable generally to private entities or individuals, as well as to Local Entities or School Districts.

(b) The Legislature shall enact statutes to establish procedures for implementing this Section consistent with the following principles and directives:

(1) The performance of functions or services not required to be performed prior to a mandate to the Local Entity or School District shall be considered a new program or increase in level of service.

(2) The increased workload under an existing program, the implementation of statutes existing at the effective date of this Article or the definition of a new crime or change in the definition of an existing crime by statute shall not be considered a mandated new program or a mandated increase in level of service.

SECTION 9. Maintenance of Local Property Tax Relief.

(a) If the State reduces local property tax relief by decreasing the specific unit amount, rate or percentage established by statute for payments made under formula to Local Entities or School Districts from that in effect upon the effective date of this Article, the State Tax Revenue Limit shall be decreased by an amount equivalent to the decrease in payments to Local Entities or School Districts.

(b) The adjustment to the State Tax Revenue Limit required by this Section shall be made in the first fiscal year of the decrease of payment described in subdivision (a) of this Section. Such adjustment shall remain in effect for each subsequent fiscal year.

SECTION 10. Adjustments for Program and Cost Transfers.

To maintain a balance between the tax burden and the cost of specific government programs at the State and local level, and to further accomplish the purposes of this Article, the Legislature shall enact statutes consistent with the following principles and directives:

(a) If the Legislature enacts a specific property tax relief measure funded by State Tax Revenues or if, by order of any court, the costs of a program are transferred from Local Entities or School Districts to the State, the State Tax Revenue Limit may be increased, providing the Maximum Property Tax Rates of affected Local Entities or the then existing tax rates of affected School Districts are commensurately decreased.

(b) If the costs of a program are transferred from the State or Local Entities or School Districts to the Federal Government, the State Revenue Limit or the Maximum Tax Rates of affected Local Entities or the then existing tax rates of affected School Districts shall be commensurately decreased.

(c) If the costs of a program are transferred to or imposed on existing or newly created Local Entities by Federal Law or the order of any court, the Maximum Property Tax Rates of affected Local Entities may be commensurately increased, pursuant to such specific conditions of State approval in each case as the Legislature may impose.

(d) If the costs of a program are transferred between existing or newly created Local Entities or School Districts, the Maximum Property Tax Rates or the then existing tax rates of each shall be commensurately adjusted.

(e) If Federal taxes are reduced on condition that the State increase expenditures by an amount equivalent to the Federal reduction, the State Tax Revenue Limit may be increased by such amount.

(f) The adjustments required by this Section of the State Tax Revenue Limit, the Maximum Property Tax Rates or the then existing tax rates in the case of School Districts shall be made in the first fiscal year of transfer or operation. Such adjustment shall remain in effect for each subsequent fiscal year.

SECTION 11. Economic Estimates Commission.

(a) There shall be an Economic Estimates Commission consisting of the State Controller; the Director of the Department of Finance or an appointee of the Governor as designated by him; and a designee appointed by the Legislature who is not a member of the Legislature, selected in a manner provided by the Joint Rules of the Legislature. The Commission shall act by a vote of two-thirds of its membership. The Commission Chairman shall be designated by the Governor. The Commission shall utilize the resources of existing State agencies in carrying out its duties.

(b) The Commission shall determine and publish, prior to April 1 of each year, the State Tax Revenue Limit for the following fiscal year by making and publishing all necessary estimates and calculations as provided in this Article. If this Amendment is not effective prior to April 1, 1974, the Commission shall determine the State Tax Revenue Limit for fiscal year 1974-75 as soon after enactment as it can act. If it does not act prior to July 1, 1974, the State Tax Revenue Limit for fiscal year 1974-75 shall be the amount of the State Tax Revenue as here defined for fiscal year 1973-74. The Commission shall also determine and publish such estimates of the State Tax Revenue Limit as are necessary for the orderly and proper development of State budgets. If the Commission does not act to determine the State Tax Revenue Limit before July 1 of a fiscal year, the State Tax Revenue Limit for that fiscal year shall remain the same as for the previous fiscal year.

SECTION 12. Computation of State Tax Revenue Limit.

(a) The State Tax Revenue Limit for a fiscal year shall be computed as the dollar sum of

(1) the greater of the following:

(i) The dollar amount derived by multiplying together the State Tax Revenue Limit Income Quotient for the specified fiscal year and the State Personal Income for the calendar year in which the specified fiscal year commences; or

(ii) The dollar amount derived by multiplying together the State Tax Revenue Limit Population-Inflation Quotient, the State Population for the calendar year in which the specified fiscal year commences and the Consumer Price Index; plus

(2) the dollar amount increase or decrease to the State Tax Revenue Limit authorized for that fiscal year pursuant to Sections 5, 9 and 10 of this Article.

(b) Beginning with the fiscal year 1989-90, or with a fiscal year in which the State Tax Revenue Limit Income Quotient is no greater than 0.0700, the Legislature, by statute passed by roll-call vote entered in the journal, two-thirds of the membership of each house concurring, may terminate further reduction in the State Tax Revenue Limit Income Quotient. Thereafter, the State Tax Revenue Limit Income Quotient shall be maintained at the level reached in the fiscal year in which such statute is enacted; however, annual reductions may be reinstated by statute passed by roll-call vote, two-thirds of the membership of each house concurring.

(c) If the statistical series used to determine the Consumer Price Index, State Personal Income and State Population, as defined in Section 16 of this Article, are recomputed by or succeeded by new series reported by the United States Department of Commerce or the United States Department of Labor or a successor agency of the United States Government, the State Tax Revenue Limit Income Quotient or State Tax Revenue Limit Population-Inflation Quotient shall be re-derived in accordance with the recomputation or new series, and the re-derived quotient shall be used in computing the State Tax Revenue Limit for the fiscal year succeeding the fiscal year in which the quotient was re-derived.

SECTION 13. Bonds and Pensions.

(a) Nothing in Section 3 or in any other provision of this Article shall limit the taxes levied or otherwise to be levied or appropriations made for the payment or discharge of any indebtedness of the State and the interest thereon heretofore or hereafter authorized by vote of the electors, or State notes or other securities issued in anticipation of the collection of taxes, and all bonds or other indebtedness of the State shall be payable from taxes of any kind or character which may be levied by the State without limitation of rate or amount.

(b) Nothing herein contained shall limit any indebtedness or liability of Local Entities or School Districts which has been duly authorized by a vote of the electors thereof. All taxes or assessments required to be levied or collected for the payment of indebtedness so incurred may be levied upon all property subject to taxation or special assessment by the Local Entities or School Districts without limit as to rate or amount, and the Maximum Property Tax Rates applicable herein shall not apply to the payment of indebtedness so incurred. The Maximum Property Tax Rates applicable to Local Entities shall not be applicable to obligations to levy taxes under the Improvement Bond Act of 1915 or to the authority of Local Entities or School Districts to levy and collect taxes to pay for Local Entities or School Districts retirement and pension benefits pursuant to laws which have been, or may in the future be, approved by the voters.

SECTION 14. Severability.

If any portion, section, subdivision or clause of this Article, or the application thereof to any entity, person or circumstance, be declared unconstitutional or held invalid or deemed unenforceable for any reason, the remaining portions of this Article and the application of such portions to other entities, persons or circumstances, shall not be affected thereby.

SECTION 15. Implementing Statutes.

(a) The Legislature, by statute, shall establish procedures for elections required by this Article, shall appropriate funds for any Statewide special election called pursuant to this Article and shall enact any other statutes necessary to carry out the provisions of this Article.

(b) The Legislature, by statute, may determine the fund or funds from which transfers to the Tax Surplus Fund, as established by subdivision (a) of Section 2 of this Article, shall be made, unless this Constitution restricts the use of a designated fund to other specified purposes. In the absence of statutory provisions, transfer to the Tax Surplus Fund shall be from the State General Fund.

SECTION 16. Definitions.

(a) "State Tax Revenue" means the revenue of the State from every tax, fee, penalty, receipt and other monetary exaction, interest in connection therewith, and any transfer out of the Tax Surplus Fund other than for tax refund, except Excluded State Revenues are not part of State Tax Revenues.

(b) "Excluded State Revenues" means

(1) The following receipts:

(i) intergovernmental transfer payments;

(ii) contributions and deposits to, receipts of, income of and proceeds of capital transactions of Employment Trust Funds;

(iii) revenue derived from a specific tax levied as permitted in Section 6 to the extent such revenue is used to meet an Emergency Situation;

(iv) proceeds from the sale or issuance of State bonds or notes;

(v) grants and contract income for projects or research sponsored and funded by non-governmental agencies;

(vi) internal fund transfers such as inter-fund or inter-agency transfers, revenue, reimbursements, abatements, advances, loans, repayment of loans;

(vii) proceeds from the sale of investments and the redemption of matured securities;

(viii) proceeds from the sale of real and personal property;

(ix) gifts, donations, bequests to the State;

(x) endowment income;

(xi) service fees and charges derived from projects which are financed by revenue bonds secured solely by the revenue of such projects to the extent that such fees and charges are used for the payment of principal and interest on such bonds;

(2) The following fees:

(i) proceeds from the activities of the University of California and the State University and College System, including, but not limited to, student tuition and fees and post-secondary education income derived from housing, parking, food service, student union fees, book stores or similar enterprises;

(ii) non-commercial fish and game fees, assessments and other revenues;

(iii) service or use fees levied by the Department of Parks and Recreation;

(iv) income from environmental license plates;

(v) revenue derived from State-owned parking lots and garages;

(3) Fees which meet all of the following criteria:

(i) the service or product for which the fee is paid is generally available from a non-State source, or the fee is collected solely to regulate a non-commercial, non-professional, non-criminal activity other than those referred to in Article XXVI;

(ii) the fee collected is used to defray all or part of the costs of the State in providing the service;

(iii) the payer of the fee receives the benefit derived from payment of the fee; and

(iv) are designated by statute as Excluded State Revenues.

(c) "Intergovernmental Transfer Payments" means dollar amounts received by the State of California from the Federal Government or any Local Entity or School District except those taxes, fees and penalties imposed by the State and collected by the Local Entity or School District for the State.

(d) "Employment Trust Funds" means the Unemployment Fund, Unemployment Administration Fund, Unemployment Compensation Disability Fund, Old Age and Survivors Insurance Revolving Fund, Uninsured Employers Fund, State Compensation Insurance Fund, State Employees Contingency Reserve Fund; and the Public Employees Retirement Fund, Teachers Retirement Fund, Judges Retirement Fund, Legislators Retirement Fund and other similar retirement funds.

(e) "Expenditure." As used herein, an expenditure occurs at the time and to the extent that a valid obligation against an appropriation is created. For the purpose of capital outlay in connection with this Article, a valid obligation shall be considered to have been incurred when the Legislature appropriates the funds.

(f) "Emergency Situation" means an extraordinary occurrence requiring unanticipated and immediate expenditures to preserve the health and safety of the people.

(g) "Maximum Property Tax Rates" means the property tax rate or rates and ad valorem special assessment rate or rates for any Local Entity.

(h) "Local Entity" means any city, county, city and county, chartered city, chartered county, chartered city and county, taxing zone, special district or other unit of government encompassing an area less than the entire State, or any Statewide district, or any combination thereof in existence on the effective date of this Article or any such entity established thereafter. Local Entity does not include a School District.

(i) "School Districts" means the entities specified as parts of the Public School System in Article IX, Section 6, of this Constitution and includes Community Colleges but does not include the State University and College System.

(j) "Estimated State Tax Revenues" means the dollar amount of State Tax Revenues as estimated by the Economic Estimates Commission.

(k) "State Personal Income" means the estimate made by the Economic Estimates Commission of the dollar amount that will be reported as Total Income by Persons for the State of California for the specified calendar year by the United States Department of Commerce or successor agency in its official publications.

(l) "State Tax Revenue Limit Income Quotient" means:

(1) For the fiscal year 1974-75, the number derived by:

(i) Dividing the sum of Estimated State Tax Revenues for the fiscal year 1973-74 by the State Personal Income for the calendar year 1973, and

(ii) Subtracting 0.001.

(2) For each fiscal year succeeding the fiscal year 1974-75, the number derived by:

(i) Dividing the State Tax Revenue Limit for the previous fiscal year by the State Personal Income for the previous calendar year, and

(ii) Subtracting 0.001.

(m) "State Population" means the estimate made by the Economic Estimates Commission of the number that will be reported as Total Population of the State of California for the specified calendar year by the United States Department of Commerce or successor agency in its official publications.

(n) "Consumer Price Index" means the number reported as the Consumer Price Index for the United States (Base Year 1967 = 100) by the United States Department of Labor, or successor agency of the United States Government, for the most current month in its latest official publication.

(o) "State Tax Revenue Limit Population-Inflation Quotient" means the number derived by dividing:

(1) The Estimated State Tax Revenue for the fiscal year 1973-74 by

(2) The State Population for the calendar year 1973 as multiplied by the Consumer Price Index available to the Economic Estimates Commission at the time it computes the State Tax Revenue Limit for fiscal year 1974-75.